"William Riley brings a light but sure touch to the task of helping readers grow in an understanding of the Scriptures. The last chapter performs a valuable service; it offers a guide for people reading the Bible on their own, a guide that selects chapters from each Scripture book to help the reader understand the great message of the Bible."

Liguorian

". . . this book examines the Bible and its history, authorship, and relevance for modern Christians. It should be helpful to beginning Bible students. . . ."

Bookstore Journal

The right book for adults who want to understand the Bible but re afraid even to try. With a clear, engaging style, the author leads ie reader through the Bible; along the way he negotiates road arriers in the minds of new readers, and is sensible enough to se a detour around problems best left for a second journey. He always alert to the humorous, and occasional cartoons add to ie flavor and convince the timid reader to plunge ahead."

The Bible Today

An attractive introduction to scripture study. It will help any teen r serious reader to find whole new dimensions in bible study."

Msgr. Charles Dollen
The Priest

When you get a copy of this book you will probably find it is book you have been looking for, for quite some time."

Intercom
Dublin, Ireland

This is exactly the book you've been looking for to put into immediate use with your high school Confirmation classes, your CIA candidates, your Bible study members and RENEW participants, your church educators, and your lay readers."

Nova
Sunday Publications

"Recommended for families, parishes, religious communities, and high schools."

"Riley's overview of the Bible is both an introduction and an invitation to the rewarding experience of reading and contemplating the Word of God. His refreshing insights will help the uninitiated discover that the Bible is truly a living book which has relevance in their daily life."

"If you want to tackle a book that is readable, entertaining and yet highly informative, you will want to put *The Tale of Two Testaments* at the top of your list. You can sow the seeds of a spiritual harvest which you can reap for a lifetime."

William Riley

THE TALE OF TWO TESTAMENTS

TWENTY-THIRD PUBLICATIONS
Mystic, Connecticut

Second printing March 1986

North American Edition 1985
Twenty-Third Publications
P.O. Box 180
Mystic CT 06355
(203) 536-2611

First Published 1985
by Veritas Publications
7-8 Lower Abbey St.
Dublin 1, Ireland

Library of Congress Catalog Card Number 85-50692
ISBN 0-89622-240-3

Contents

Introduction

MOST Christians at some time or another feel that they should know a bit more about the Bible. (Those who feel that they know it all already are usually the ones to avoid!) But the very size of the task can appear so great that often nothing ever comes of even the best intentions.

This book is both an invitation and an introduction to the rewarding experience of God's Word. It presumes no prior training or experience, though hopefully those with a limited knowledge of the Bible would deepen it through reading these pages. Most of the individual chapters concentrate on major sections of the Bible, approaching them from the standpoint of modern biblical study which has deepened our appreciation of Scripture's richness and relevance.

Brevity has been a concern throughout, and while this might help the reader to get an overview of the Bible quickly, it does have its disadvantages. Interesting questions get ignored or glossed over lightly. Areas of scholarly debate cannot have all points of view presented. Some of the biblical books are not treated at all to afford more space to those that are. But these limitations are inevitable if a book is to be suited to those who are making the first uneasy steps along an unfamiliar road.

After finishing this book, the reader will not be a biblical scholar. But he or she will certainly have some idea of what the scriptures are saying and how they say it. Perhaps the biblical readings heard on Sundays will become a little more intelligible; perhaps the Bible will come to be seen as a tome more to be read than to be dusted. Perhaps readers will discover that the Bible is their book, part of their heritage as members of the family of God.

Finally, I would like to thank Veritas Publications for their involvement in this book from the concept's initial spark to the printed work. Gratitude must also be expressed to my friends and colleagues who read the manuscript and offered their suggestions: especially Sister Carmel McCarthy of the Religious Education

Department, Carysfort College of Education, Father Shán Ó Cuív, and Theo Payne who was also involved with the artwork for the book. To these, and to all of those who have given their encouragement, co-operation and advice, I owe my sincerest thanks.

The Book of Books

BEYOND APPEARANCES

THE old man's voice faded to a whisper and his audience leaned a little closer to catch the climax of his tale. He was telling a story about their common ancestors and a trick played on an old man by his clever wife. The heroine of his story was a woman named Rebekah, the mother of Jacob who was the great ancestor of the nation; every listener knew that the fate of their nation depended on how that story ended.

With the royal wedding in only a few days, poetic inspiration had to come quickly to the court composer. He pitied the poor bride in a way, being married to someone she hardly knew, having to move to a different country; it could be hard being a king's daughter and subject to marriage as international politics demanded! But then, wasn't she going to lead a privileged life at the court of the great King of Judah? Maybe she was luckier than she might realise. The royal composer wrote a new verse for the wedding song; it began: "Listen, daughter ... forget your people and your father's house and the king will desire your beauty."

It was heartbreaking, without a doubt. To think that he had worked so long and so hard among these people, and now they were abandoning everything that he had taught them to follow some legalistic nonsense with a Christian veneer. Paul decided that it was time for some straight talking; he only hoped that his heated words wouldn't set the papyrus alight.

IT would undoubtedly come as quite a surprise to any of the people in these three scenarios, but they had one thing in common: they were all writing the Bible. They lived in different centuries, and spoke different languages, but the words which they put together would some day be printed between the same covers for people of every imaginable race and language and age.

All sorts of people made their contribution to the Bible. Scriptural writers weren't all prophets preaching in the Temple or apostles writing to errant young churches; the Bible contains just about every kind of writing from love songs to short stories. There is even an ancient detective thriller lurking at the end of the Book of Daniel!

When a modern Christian holds a Bible, there is a small library of seventy-three books in his or her hands.[1] The material in that library has been gathered over thirteen centuries and translated from three different languages. As we might expect in any library, the books of the Bible show different outlooks and approaches reflecting different interests and different problems.

Most of us have a straightforward picture of how books come into existence: the author writes a manuscript which is sent to a publisher who produces a book. The history of biblical books departs from such a picture in several ways: few of the biblical books had a single author; much of the material in them circulated for years or even generations before it was ever committed to writing. Even the process of deciding which books should be included in the Bible was long and complex and its history is a study on its own.

The Bible had to pass along a lengthy assembly line before it came to us. At the beginning of the line are the storytellers and poets, historians and letter writers and all the others who framed Scripture's words and phrases. Somewhere further down the line come the Jewish and Christian scribes who copied the text for centuries, producing the manuscripts so important to biblical scholars today. Then, as the needs of people demanded, the

---

1. Throughout this book, the biblical books are treated as they are found in Catholic bibles. The difference between Catholic and most non-Catholic bibles only affects the contents of the Old Testament. The books of Tobit, Judith, Wisdom, Sirach, Baruch and First and Second Maccabees do not appear in the non-Catholic Old Testament and the books of Esther and Daniel are somewhat shorter.

translators set to work. Certain specialists made their own contribution, too, such as the bishop who divided the Bible into chapters in the Middle Ages and the person who subdivided the chapters into verses in Reformation times. In strictly human terms, putting the Bible together required an enormous workforce.

More than simply Human

But few people read Scripture out of a purely human interest. Christians believe that these books, as well as being thoroughly human, are thoroughly divine. They reflect what God wants to tell us as no other writing does. We even call these books 'The Word of God', a title that we give to Christ himself, for when Scripture is read, especially as part of the Church's worship, Christians hear the voice of Jesus speaking to them.[2]

Now we might well expect a different book from God. We might expect the book to consist of clearly written, fact-filled articles which are easy to use and which do not admit of ambiguities. If this is to be our basic sourcebook for such an important thing as what God wants to tell us and what God expects from us, if the Bible is going to act as the Christian's rule book for the game of life, then the least we could hope for is cut-and-dried precision and clarity. And with this reasonable expectation in mind, when we first open the Bible, what do we find? All stories and poems and letters and proverbs! And we feel like suggesting to God that he could have produced a much shorter work if only he had stuck to the point.

What God is actually doing is using every possible means to tell us about himself and his plan for us. The Bible was never meant to be an encyclopaedia of facts, but an invitation. Through the Bible, God shows himself to humanity as a lover; and through Scripture, we discover how to respond to that invitation and enter into an ever-deepening relationship with the Revealer.

Scripture is all about religious truth, the truth which God has given us to lead us to salvation.[3] That is the only kind of truth that we are guaranteed to find in Scripture. This is obvious to any student of the Bible who sees that Scripture isn't afraid of

2. *Introduction to the Roman Lectionary,* paragraphs 4 and 10.
3. The Second Vatican Council, *Dei Verbum,* paragraph 11.

Is the Bible a rule book for the game of life?

contradicting itself in small matters such as the family tree of a central figure or the details of a story; sometimes a biblical writer will consciously amend a story which he has borrowed from an earlier writer. If it were the purpose of the Word of God to give us factual records of the past, such contradictions would never occur. And the person who claims that they don't has either never read the whole of the Bible or has read it with great inattention!

The Bible and History

Once upon a time — and not so long ago — most people in the Western world believed that everything in the Bible was true in every conceivable sense. But Darwin's theories of the origin of the species and archaeological discoveries seemed to make such a belief more and more untenable. Even so, an important question for many modern readers remains: "Can I believe what I read in the Bible?" And, as with most questions worth asking, the answer is not as simple as we would like it to be.

Firstly, we must admit that we once read parts of Scripture with the presumption that every story in it was written as history (though we did make an exception for the parables). Yet much of this material was intended for different purposes altogether, as has been shown by a closer comparison of these writings with other ancient literature. Now that we know that the Adam and Eve story was written to give us insight into human nature and its failings rather than as an account of prehistory, we can read it with a greater appreciation of its original message. Much the same would be true of other writings in the Old Testament, such as Jonah, Job and Judith — though with slight differences in each case. Our modern insights come largely from learning to ask the question "What kind of literature was the original author trying to produce?" The answers to that question have shed light on just about every corner of the Bible.

Secondly, we cannot fail to recognise that much of the Bible is indeed concerned with history; but we would be mistaken to presume that the historical concerns of the biblical authors were the same as the concerns of modern historians. Today there are methods of research and critical standards for the historian which were simply unknown in the ancient world. Perhaps more importantly, the ancient historian had a different concept of what history is about. Sometimes this is expressed through the equation:

$$\text{History} = \text{Facts} + \text{Interpretation}$$

Certainly, facts are central to history, but unless those facts are interpreted, the historian has done nothing but produce a clutter of statistics. In our approach to history, we place a definite emphasis on facts; the ancients placed a greater emphasis on the interpretation of events. The modern historian asks questions like "Who?", "Where?" "When?" "How?"; the ancient historian was far more interested in asking "Why?"

Consequently, since the biblical historians were people of their time and culture, they were trying to uncover and reveal the meaning of the past rather than its factual details. Other differences also emerge; for instance, if two different accounts of the same incident came into the biblical historian's hands, he was likely to incorporate both into his final work — sometimes giving the modern reader the impression that something happened twice in slightly different ways! Modern historians, of course, would try to give a unified account by deciding what was factual in each of the sources. With different methods and a different philosophy of history behind their methods, the biblical historians were bound to produce a far different result from that demanded by the modern reader of the historians of his own age.

The biblical historians, by and large, saw it as their responsibility to trace God's involvement with his people. The God of Scripture is hardly the immutable God of the Greek philosophers who seems to dwell in a region beyond the ages, untouched by the affairs of time-bound humanity. The God of the Bible is quite busy with human affairs, using the flow of Israel's history to deepen and develop his relationship with his people.

Whatever befell them, be it prosperity or calamity, Israel learned to see it as God at work, blessing or reproving, warning or encouraging — all through the events of Israel's history.

And when Israel wanted to think about God, they often did it by reflecting on where their history was going and how it had taken shape so far.

The Old Testament name for God encapsulated the Hebrew's awareness of God's role in history. That name is "Yahweh",[4] and there are two possible ways of putting that name into English. The first is to translate it as "He is there" or simply "He is", a statement that at every turn of Israel's history, God was with his people, at every time and in every place. But the other way of translating the sacred name is even more awesome: "He who causes to be", "He who makes things happen". And, indeed, that is precisely what Yahweh proved to be for the Israelites: the source and guiding force of all their history.

Even in historiography, the Bible's concern is religious; everything else is secondary. And when we read the books of Scripture, we must respect its priorities; unless our prime concern lies in its religious message, we are demanding that it change its purpose for us. Whether our demand be dramatic impact or poetic beauty or historical accuracy or a chronicle of cosmogony, we are

4. The name Yahweh became so sacred to the Old Testament people that it fell out of everyday use altogether. Instead of pronouncing the sacred name when they were reading the Old Testament aloud, the reader would say "Adonai" which means "the Lord". Most Christian bibles follow this practice and print "LORD" whenever "Yahweh" occurs in the original text. The name Yahweh never occurs as such in the New Testament, a further indication of how rarely it was spoken by the first century of the Christian era. The pronunciation "Jehovah" is a mistaken attempt to read the divine name as it appears in the Hebrew Bible. It is undoubtedly erroneous and best forgotten.

opening ourselves to possible disappointment, for **we are** demanding something which Scripture never promised **to give us.**

But the Bible does make other claims for itself, substantial claims. It promises to unfold for us the story of God and humanity in an ever-deepening way. It shows us how humanity moved from darkness and ignorance by gradual advances into the shining light of Christ. And it even promises to be a beam of that light for those who read it today.

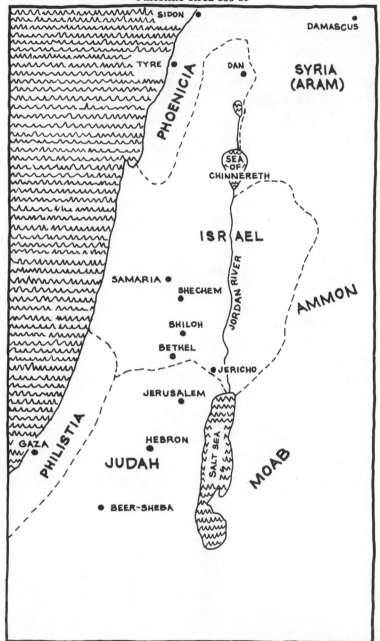

Palestine circa 800 BC

The Story of a People

HALF A DOZEN AGES IN AS MANY PAGES

ONE of the major problems which faces the beginning reader of Scripture is the Old Testament's assumption that everyone is familiar with the history of Israel. The simple fact is that many a modern reader would be hard-pressed to give the barest outline of even the major events of the Old Testament. These few pages will provide just such an outline for the sake of those who have perhaps heard reference made to the exodus and the exile and the period of the monarchy, but who aren't quite certain as to how they fit together.

Looking at the Sources

The writings of the Old Testament themselves provide us with most of our information about the ancient history of Israel. Some of the books of the Old Testament seem to be largely concerned with relating part of the nation's history, and so are often referred to as the "Historical Books".[1] Sometimes parts of other Old Testament books also give us information about what was happening in those ancient days. Although archaeology and the writings of Israel's neighbours allow the experts to reconstruct Israel's history with more precision than has been possible for centuries, the starting point is always the Bible's own record, how Israel gives its account of events both momentous and minor.

Three groups of books provide us with most of the Old Testament story. Each group represents the end product of a long

---

1. The term "Historical Books" can be confusing if we assume that the Old Testament writers shared the concerns and standards of the modern historian. See Chapter One of this book.

process which involved the bringing together of material from many different sources; and although the three groups share a common conviction that Yahweh was at the centre of Israel's history, each also has characteristics which set it apart from the others. These three main groupings are:

1. *The Torah,* or Pentateuch, undoubtedly the most important five books in the Old Testament. They trace the story of Israel from its beginning to the time when the people entered the Promised Land. The books in the Torah are: Genesis, Exodus, Leviticus, Numbers and Deuteronomy; much more will be said about them in Chapter Three.

2. *The Deuteronomic History,* so called by scholars because its interpretation is heavily influenced by the Book of Deuteronomy. These books stress that following God's Law brought blessings to his people, and disobeying the commandments always brought disaster. The importance of the Temple in Jerusalem and the necessity of a king who dedicated himself to observing the demands of the law were among the other major interests of these books.

   The writings of the deuteronomic historians include: Joshua, Judges, First and Second Samuel and First and Second Kings. These books supply most of our information about the period from the time the people entered the Promised Land to the Exile.

3. *The Chronicler's History* used the work of the deuteronomic historians, but placed far more emphasis on the Temple and its worship and far less on the importance of the king. First and Second Chronicles, certainly part of the Chronicler's history, begin with genealogical listings of the families of Israel and then proceed to trace the story of the kingdom of Judah until the return from Exile. Ezra and Nehemiah are usually included as part of the Chronicler's history; both of those books are concerned with Judah's efforts to rebuild itself after the disaster of the Exile.

Largely relying on the picture painted by these sources, the next few pages will give a brief, bare outline of the major eras and events of the Old Testament period as seen by the Old Testament itself. Many of the dates mentioned are only approximate.

The Age of the Patriarchs

At the opening of Israel's history, there were no Israelites at all, no chosen people, no one who knew God. Then, from all the people on the earth, Yahweh chose *Abraham* and his wife *Sarah*, an elderly childless couple who were resigned to facing the grave without anyone to carry on the family line. Such a prospect was even more serious for Abraham and Sarah than it would be for a Christian couple today, because they lacked any idea of life after death; descendants were about the only type of continued existence that people could look forward to. So when Yahweh called Abraham, he held out to him the promise of a son whose own descendants would form the nation of Israel. Abraham's problems didn't end there by any means, and the child took a few years to come along, but his story (shocking at times, inspiring at others) stands as proof that faith is an adventure. Eventually the son, *Isaac,* is born, and he

Many early historic figures are shrouded in the mists of time.

in turn has a son, *Jacob*. There is something of the rogue in Jacob, a twister who cheats his brother Esau of his inheritance (and who is himself cheated once or twice). Jacob has twelve sons who, in turn, are seen as the ancestors of the Twelve Tribes of the Old Testament people. The solidarity which the later nation felt with their ancestors can be seen in the name which they gave themselves: Israel, the other name given to their common ancestor Jacob.

These early stages in Israel's history are well shrouded in the mists of time, and much of what we have in the ancestral stories of Genesis is more the work of the storyteller than the work of the historians. Abraham, Isaac and Jacob are depicted as landless nomads — the type of people whose story is to be found in folklore rather than in carefully documented biographies. It is even difficult to date their era, although it seems a reasonable estimation to say that the years between 1800 and 1700 BC witnessed some of their days.

Joseph is the last of the ancestral figures to play a major part in these narratives. The stories about him make a good read, and that is possibly part of the reason that they have found their way into the Bible. His story explains how the descendants of Abraham migrated from Palestine into the land of Egypt where the next act of the biblical drama is staged.

The Exodus
The Book of Exodus opens with a scene of forgetfulness: a new king of Egypt who had forgotten all that Joseph had done for the Egyptians centuries before, many descendants of Jacob and his sons who had all but forgotten the great God of their ancestors. Instead of the Hebrews being the honoured guests of the Pharaoh (as was the case at the end of Genesis), we find them groaning under the burdens of slavery. The story of their liberation under the leadership of *Moses* also tells the story of Yahweh's fundamental revelation of himself to his people: who he is, what his promises to Israel are, what his demands for Israel are.

Much of what Israel discovered about God during the Exodus (the "going out" from Egypt, sometime around 1250 BC) is summed up by their realisation that they had a *covenant* with their

God. Covenant may not be a very meaningful term to us, but it was an everyday word for the ancient Hebrews; it was a way of making a solemn agreement which also brought the people involved into a very close (and nearly unbreakable) relationship. The laws given through Moses would not have been seen as autocratic regulations from on high; rather, they were Israel's part of the bargain, the way that Israel would express their attachment to Yahweh in this unique relationship.

The idea of covenant is one of the central pillars on which all the Old Testament's religious awareness rests. Even though there are several important covenants spoken of in the Old Testament (such as the one with Abraham or the one with David), in the Hebrew scriptures the term usually refers to the covenant made through Moses.[2]

The Conquest and Period of the Judges
Eventually, the Israelites arrived at their goal, the "Promised Land". The Bible gives us two pictures of how the Chosen People took possession of it: the Book of *Joshua* gives the picture of a triumphant sweeping conquest; the Book of *Judges* records a slower progress, a mixture of small victories and large setbacks. The difference is easily explained: Joshua is a noble epic meant to celebrate the great gift of the land; Judges is probably that bit nearer to the real picture. The judges themselves were not to be found in the courtrooms but on the battlefields. They are called "judges" because they vindicated the rights of Israel against their oppressors (although a passage like Judg 4:4-5 would indicate that the courtroom would not have been totally alien to them). It was — despite the strong personalities of the judges — a time of distress and often of disunity for the Israelites; these Old Testament Dark Ages lasted from about 1200 BC to almost 1000 BC.

The United Monarchy
A generation before the end of the period of the judges, the figure of *Samuel* appeared. He might be pictured as a judge at times, a prophet at others, but his most important role in history was that

---

2. Often referred to as the Sinai Covenant after the place where it was made. More is said about this covenant in Chapter Three.

of kingmaker. The people of Israel demanded a king, their many political, religious and economic reasons being expressed in Scripture's succinct phrase, "like all the other nations".

Samuel anointed *Saul* as king — as half-king, really, for he had few of the powers or privileges of an ancient king and was kept very much under Samuel's thumb. When Saul proved unsatisfactory, Samuel appointed *David* as king, although David only really became a ruler after the death of Samuel and Saul. His reign was long (about 1000-961 BC) and eventful. The story of his time on the throne includes many wars, the most notable being against his own son Absalom who tried to depose him. In the books of Samuel the figure of David is drawn larger than life as a man of powerful strengths and tragic weaknesses.

King David made two outstanding and lasting contributions to the story of Israel. The first was the conquest of Jerusalem, a city which belonged to the Jebusites. By making Jerusalem his capital, David surmounted tribal rivalries by using a city which had not been associated with any particular tribe. By bringing the Ark of the Covenant (the Old Testament symbol of Yahweh's presence) into his new capital, David also made Jerusalem the religious centre of the nation, the city where Yahweh made his home in the human world.

David's second contribution was the establishment of a dynasty. In 2 Sam 7:1-17, Scripture presents this as a gift from God to David; it was also very much a gift to the nation, for it guaranteed a relatively stable government when the alternative to rule by dynasty was rule by social upheaval and assassination. The promise of a dynasty to David was the basis for the Messianic hope of later generations.[3]

David's son, *Solomon,* also had a great list of achievements to his credit. During his reign, Israel became more involved in international affairs. Solomon seems to have reigned over a small empire, and the size of his sphere of influence is indicated by the large number of his foreign wives (a royal marriage to a foreign princess was a standard way of establishing or consolidating

3. 'Messiah' comes from a Hebrew word which means 'The Anointed One' (kings were appointed through a ceremony of anointing). "Christ" has exactly the same meaning although it derives from a Greek word.

diplomatic ties). David may have brought the Ark to Jerusalem, but Solomon built the Temple to house it, the Temple which would be be the centre of the religious life of Israel for a thousand years — and which would feature in the life of Jesus.[4]

The Divided Kingdom

Solomon's reign may have been prosperous, but that did not necessarily make it popular. The tribes of the North felt that they had too large a share of Solomon's expenses and too small a share of his benefits. After his death, the northern tribes broke away (around 922 BC) and the period of the divided kingdom began. The

Solomon's reign wasn't popular with the Northern Tribes.

4. The Temple which stood in Jerusalem during the time of Jesus was on the same site as Solomon's Temple, but was Herod's renovation of a building erected in the sixth century BC.

northern kingdom was called *Israel,* the southern kingdom was called *Judah* (after the tribe which made up most of its population).

The history of these two petty kingdoms is largely overwritten by the superpowers of the day, especially Egypt, Assyria and (later) Babylon. Both Israelite nations had their moments of glory and their hours of distress, sometimes acting as allies, and at other times as enemies. During this period, the prophets came into prominence with their unheeded warning that moral decadence —especially in the northern kingdom of Israel, but also in the southern kingdom of Judah — was undermining the social fabric of the state and endangering its very survival.

The northern kingdom fell in 722 BC when its capital city, Samaria, surrendered to the Assyrian invaders.[5] Much of the population of the northern kingdom was exiled from the land of Israel and a mixed population was settled there instead. After a few generations of intermarriage (both in the places of exile and in the former northern kingdom of Israel), all ethnic identity was lost. The only remaining trace was the hated race of Samaritans, looked upon as spiritual and genetic half-breeds by their fiercely nationalistic neighbours in Judah. Intermarriage had resulted in the disappearance of the "Ten Lost Tribes" in the melting pot of the Assyrian Empire.

After the fall of the northern kingdom, there were two outstanding kings of Judah (and quite a few of the usual type as well). These were *Hezekiah* (715-687 BC) and *Josiah* (640-609 BC); both were reformers, hoping to rebuild Judah politically and religiously. Josiah's religious reform was fuelled by the discovery of what is known to us as the Book of Deuteronomy (or its key sections) during a restoration of the Temple. Both reformations were only skin deep, and after the death of the reforming monarchs it was business as usual.

The Babylonian Exile

A new superpower was looming, the Neo-Babylonian Empire. Judah, having been a vassal of an old superpower, Egypt, could

5. Israel's doom was on the cards for quite a few years before this. When Israel's armies were putting pressure on the King of Judah, he appealed to Assyria for help — which Assyria was only too pleased to provide.

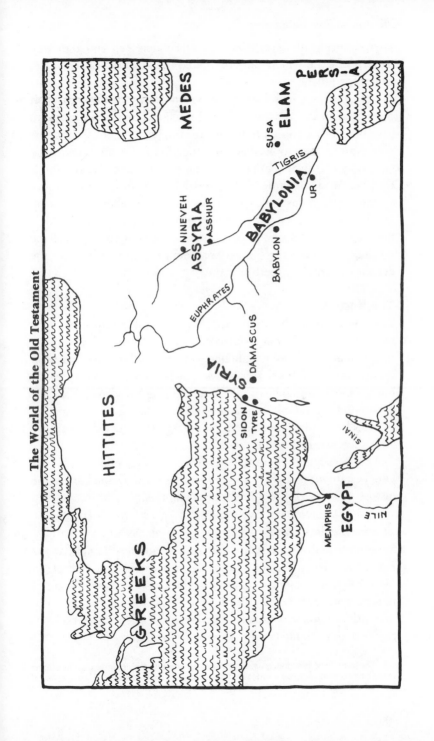

The World of the Old Testament

start counting its days. In 587 BC, Jerusalem fell and the same pattern of exile which had obliterated the kingdom of Israel had begun for Judah.

Perhaps they had learned a lesson from the fate of their northern cousins, for this period of the Babylonian exile seems to have been remarkably productive for the Jews.[6] Cut off from the worship of the Temple, they met together for common worship and study on the Sabbath (the beginnings of synagogue worship); they began to put some of their older oral traditions into a more definite form; constant exposure to the pagan belief and worship around them sharpened their awareness of the one-ness of God. It must have seemed like a last desperate attempt to stave off the inevitable, to preserve the national identity when faced with the devouring, grinding teeth of exile.

The Restoration

Then what must have seemed like a miracle happened: the Babylonian Empire was overthrown by the Persians, who had a policy of allowing the people under them to follow their national traditions in their home territories. The Jews in Babylon were sent home, and under figures like *Ezra* the priest and *Nehemiah* the governor they rebuilt Jerusalem and its Temple and began life again. The restoration started around 538 BC, just half a century after the exile had begun.

This is roughly where the Hebrew scriptures end. The Greek Old Testament is slightly longer than the Hebrew and carries the history of Israel on for a few more centuries.

The Hellenistic Age

Superpowers do not last forever, so it is not surprising that the Persian Empire gave way to the armies of Alexander the Great (356 — 323 BC). Alexander's empire soon broke up into three smaller, but sizeable units; the culture which became nearly universal under their domain is usually referred to as Hellenistic (Greekish) rather than Hellenic (purely Greek).

6. The term "Jew" is properly used only from the time of the exile since it has its origins in the term used to describe a Judaean. To call a member of a northern tribe a Jew would have all the inaccuracy of calling a Scotsman an Englishman.

One of the Hellenistic emperors under whose sway Judaea fell was Antiochus IV, a man determined to bring Palestine into the full swing of the Hellenistic way of life: the Jews were required to worship the Greek gods and to abandon their ancestral way of life. Many Jews, of course, complied. After all, it must have seemed to some of them to be simply a matter of catching up with the rest of the world. But others resisted under the leadership of the *Maccabees* in 167 BC. Three years later, they celebrated their success with a rededication of the Temple which had been profaned by Hellenistic rituals. It was an amazing accomplishment.

Although it is not mentioned in the Old Testament, there was one final, and fatal, interference in Jewish affairs. Alliances with *Rome* were formed in the days following the Maccabean revolt, but it was in 63 BC that the real Roman domination began. Rome, in the person of Pompey, appointed itself arbitrator in a dispute between two brothers over who should accede to the throne and high priesthood. From that time forward political powers in Palestine were the puppets of Rome until the events of the first and second centuries after Christ which snuffed out the political existence of Judaea like a candle.

That completes the overview of Israel's history which such a small amount of space permits. If you want the fire and spirit, the lessons and the mystery of Israel's story, you will have to go to those pages where Israel's historians have pondered the who and why of their saga — and discovered God.

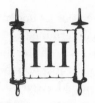

Books of Identity

THE TORAH

MANY a beginning Bible reader has begun with the notion of reading the whole volume from start to finish. The object: to have read the whole of Scripture. The method: to open the book at Genesis chapter one, verse one and to continue in an orderly fashion until the last page of the Book of Revelation is finished. The result: disaster. The good intentions receive a battering in the table of nations in Genesis ten, are fatally wounded by the rules in Exodus, but might limp courageously on until the coup-de-grace of the Book of Leviticus and its concerns with ritual. If you are tempted by such a course of action, the best advice to give to you is "Don't!" The biblical books were not written in the order in which they appear, nor were they meant to be read in that order. The list of books which appears at the front of your bible is a valuable table of contents, but disastrous as a reading plan.[1]

At the same time, there are certain reasons for the order of appearance of the books of the Bible. The Old/New Testament division is obvious enough — the first represents our common heritage with the people of Israel, the latter contains the books sacred to us specifically as Christians. But then there are smaller divisions within these which are just as logical; and within the Old Testament, the most important of these groupings is made up of the first five biblical books: Genesis, Exodus, Leviticus, Numbers and Deuteronomy.

---

1. See Chapter Eleven for suggestions as to what to read when beginning to explore the Bible.

Law or Instruction?

There are two usual ways to refer to these books as a group. Sometimes they are called the *Pentateuch,* which is simply a Greek way of saying "the five books" (or five scrolls, to be more exact); but they are also referred to by their Hebrew title, *Torah,* which we often translate into English as "the Law".

No one could deny that these books contain a number of laws (over 600 according to the traditional reckoning), yet most scholars are unhappy with "law" as a translation of *torah.* For one thing, there is much material in these books which isn't law at all. There are stories about creation, about ancient Abraham, about the coming out of Egypt, about the wanderings in the desert. Perhaps a more important reason is the negative overtones which the word "law" has for modern ears: we can too often think of law as something arbitrary and inconvenient. Any positive attitudes which we possess towards law are shallow enough to be blown away by the sight of a parking ticket neatly tucked under our windscreen wiper.

Besides, the Hebrew term *torah* is itself wider than just law; it also embraces such ideas as guidance and advice. It was a word to describe what you were given when you talked over your problem with someone else, or the light thrown on a decision which you had brought to God in prayer. So, if some English equivalent for *torah* is needed, the best of all seems to be the word "instruction".

The Torah gives its instruction in more than one way. Certainly many specific situations were addressed by its rules and regulations, and this was a very definite form of instruction. But more important than the details, the Torah was meant to instruct through the vision of life which it imparts to its readers. Like most of the books of the Bible, the Torah was meant to be read again and again, to sink into the very hearts of its hearers. If the individual laws were fashioned to govern different aspects of life, the Torah as a whole is fashioned to give life a certain meaning and direction. The stories of Abraham and Sarah present an example of trust in Yahweh, the problems of doubts and trials, the ultimate vindication of belief against the odds. Other stories, such as those about Noah or creation, show that God is concerned with the whole of humanity, not just with Israel, his special possession. The

29

saga of the Exodus displays the Lord's concern with the problems of his people and his power to save.

The detailed rules and regulations hold only an historical interest for Christians now; the New Testament impresses on us time and again that these are no longer binding for those who believe in Christ. Yet the vision of life which we find in the Torah is as valid for us as it was for the ancient Hebrews, and the New Testament refers to that vision again and again. In fact, the careful reader will find over 800 quotations from the Torah in the New Testament pages!

The New Testament writers might have felt liberated from the restrictive regulations of the Torah, yet they recognised that these books still had tremendous importance for the Christian vision. It is because the Torah contains the stories about the beginnings of Yahweh's dealings with humanity that it holds its central place. As an acorn contains the oak, the Torah tells us the most important things about God and our response to him, even though their full importance cannot be seen except in the light of Christ. The Israelites looked here for the foundation stories of their relationship with Yahweh, and — because we are spiritually the descendants of the Israelites — we turn to these pages with a similar goal in mind.

The Exodus Story

Four out of the five books of the Torah deal with the saga which brings the people of Israel out of slavery up to the threshold of the Promised Land. Such volume of space devoted to this story is proof of its importance for the Old Testament people. The Exodus marked the transformation of Israel from a clan to a nation, from subservience to self-determination. This was the time when Yahweh set Israel on their feet and showed them the way to walk; how well they followed the advice is, as the saying goes, another story.

There is considerable debate among scholars as to what actually happened at the Exodus. Such questions arise because we have no ancient reference to the liberation of Israel from Egypt outside of the biblical records, and the biblical records themselves present us with a few questions of their own. One of the more famous problems of the pentateuchal account is that it gives more than one account of the route which the people took from Egypt to Canaan.

Of course, we will never know precisely what happened at this decisive time. The biblical authors knew that they were not simply dealing with the banalities of history but with a veritable mystery of faith. By the time our records began to take their present form they were ornamented by the storyteller and the poet. As these stories were told and retold, they accumulated the religious insights of later ages. Changed customs and practices were seen to have the same standing as earlier ones and so became part of the law given to Moses. The end result is a story woven from many different strands, containing within it the very heart of Israel's belief and relationship to God.

Some parts of the Exodus story deserve special mention. After a brief introduction to the plight of the Hebrews and the early life of Moses, Yahweh introduces himself into Israelite history. This was to be the beginning of an involvement by God in the history of his people which would be chronicled in the pages of the Old Testament for a thousand years and more. How does the book of Exodus capture the magnitude of this event? When all memory of God had vanished, the reminder came to Moses from a burning bush. God gave no doctrinal formulae or mystical experiences; the entire interview was couched in the type of language that Moses could readily understand — God promised to bring the Hebrews out of slavery. And the guarantee that God would bind himself to the enslaved Israelites might well be seen in what else he told Moses — his name, "Yahweh" — for, according to the ancient way of thinking, the revelation of the name of a god brought people into special intimacy with that god.

What follows is a powerful saga: Moses goes to Pharaoh with his demands, and obstinate Pharaoh is worn down by the famous ten plagues. Often the modern reader misses the drama of this scene. With our cosy assumption that there can only be one God, we forget that the Egyptians (and all other ancient peoples) believed in many gods, and Pharaoh was, in a sense, one of those gods. So before the Israelites could be free, there had to be a divine battle, a struggle between the two deities, Yahweh and Pharaoh, until one was vanquished. Our theology might be more refined,

Obstinate Pharaoh being worn down by the ten plagues.

but the ancient theology made for better stories!

The tenth plague brought the liberation and the first Passover feast. There is now general agreement that the Passover meal goes back to rituals far more ancient than the Exodus, but all of the meaning of its foods and rituals are now traced back to the night when the first-born were slain.[2]

The final victory of Yahweh over Pharaoh was yet to come at the Red Sea, or Sea of Reeds as it is more accurately called. Again, the historical events must be forever submerged beneath the Exodus traditions like the Egyptian chariots in the Cecil B. De Mille epic. Whether you prefer to picture walls of water standing like tower blocks to form a guard of honour for the fleeing Israelites or the more modern image of a marsh temporarily dried

---

2. A closer look at Passover will be taken in Chapter Four.

out by the effects of strong winds, the significance of the events at the Sea of Reeds remains the same in the biblical outlook: now Israel is truly liberated, free once and for all from its Egyptian overlords.

A free people indeed, but can we yet refer to Israel as a nation? Really they were little more than a wandering band led by the charismatic figure of Moses. Most of those factors which would make Israel a nation (such as laws, structures and the land in which they would settle) were a result of the covenant at Sinai.

We rarely use the word covenant anymore, yet it was an important element in the ordinary lives of this ancient people. As an institution, covenant comes down from the days when writing was a highly specialised skill, perhaps harking back to the days when writing wasn't known at all. When two parties wanted to make a solemn agreement, they entered covenant, which meant that they guaranteed that the terms of their agreement would be kept by calling on the gods to witness it and to enforce it, killing an animal to demonstrate what would happen to the party who broke the terms, and entering into a firm relationship which also helped to ensure that the agreement would be kept. Naturally, from such simple beginnings, the covenant came to have more than one form and one application. Sometimes individuals would enter covenant to enshrine their special relationship, like the covenant of friendship between David and Jonathan. Even after the craft of writing became more widespread, kings would enter covenant as a means of making treaties between their peoples, often recording the event on tablets. Covenants seem to have been as much a part of life in these times as contracts are in our own.

Chapters nineteen to twenty-four of Exodus record the covenant at Sinai. Most of it makes strange, and sometimes off-putting reading to the modern Christian, yet the unique event which is to be found there forms one of the cornerstones of the Old Testament and has great echoes in the New. The main body of this section (Ex 20-23) follows the usual broad outline for treaties between kings, so there are no real surprises in the structure of this covenant. What *is* outstanding is that covenants were not usually made by deities. When Yahweh made covenant at Sinai, he was not simply giving his people a law code to form the basis of their nation, he was drawing them to himself in the type of intimate relationship which existed between no other people and their gods.

The covenant relationship was often spoken of with two special words, sometimes translated as *loving kindness* and *faithfulness*. The strength and intimacy of this relationship was to be realised more and more by God's people until, through people like the prophet Hosea, it could only be compared with marriage. The blood of the covenant animal, once shed as a warning to the covenant partners, becomes in Exodus a symbol of the one life now shared between Yahweh and his people.

Perhaps no concept is more central to the biblical understanding of God and his relationship with his people than covenant, with its emphasis on tender love and solid responsibilities. Although there is more than one covenant in the Old Testament (as we shall see), the term usually refers to the covenant at Sinai, since that was where Yahweh made this people his own. Nor can we confine covenant to the pages of the Old Testament; according to the gospels, Jesus looked upon his death as establishing a new covenant in which his lifeblood links his followers to the Father, a covenant which we renew at the Eucharist. The concept should still be central for Christians today.

The rest of Exodus, as well as Leviticus and Numbers, continues the story from Sinai to the Promised Land. Deuteronomy belongs in a category of its own. It is a later restatement of the Torah, which places far more emphasis on a person's interior values than on exterior actions. The Israelite is not only given norms of behaviour, but is urged to keep the principles which lay behind them always in mind, delving deeper into them through contemplation and discussion. New emphasis on the free choice of the hearer is also to be found, with stern reminders that these choices have consequences. At the end of the book, the days of Moses' leadership end with the story of his death and burial.

The Ancestral Stories

Even though we can look upon the liberation from Egypt as a real beginning for Israel's relationship with God, the Old Testament people knew that God had never been a stranger to them. They traced Yahweh's involvement with them right back to the ancestors of their race. If we expect these ancestral stories (which are to be found in chapters twelve to fifty of Genesis) to make consistently inspirational reading, we are bound for disappointment. The modern reader is met with tales of trickery, envy, near-fratricide and marital customs which offend Christian sensibilities. In other words, much of the material which we now find in Genesis was not originally intended to be religious, but to provide interesting stories about common ancestors. Families still indulge in this past-time, so that we all have the experience of knowing much about the personalities of relatives whom we have never met and of whom we have no personal recollection. So too, the attentive reader of these ancestral tales will soon discern the strong personalities of the main characters: Abraham, the first to discover that faith could bring you trouble as well as blessing; resourceful Rebekah, who managed to turn the destinies of her sons upside down; crafty Jacob, from whom one would be afraid to buy a used donkey; and Joseph, who matures from naïve arrogance into amazing sensitivity.

Despite the non-religious quality of many of these tales, clear religious messages come across. The most striking of these is Yahweh's careful nurturing of his people from their earliest development, a theme very consistent with the Bible's whole outlook on the history of Israel. Other lesser themes also emerge, such as the promises of God and their fulfilment, or the ancestors' connection with places which would gain importance in the later religious life of Israel.

The outstanding lesson to be learned from the ancestral stories according to the New Testament is taught by Abraham, the first of these gigantic figures. He is a wealthy nomad, who responds to God's call by doing what he knows best: moving on to the land that God would show him. The promise was straightforward, a son to a childless couple, complicated only by the great age of those who received the promise. Part of the attraction of the Abraham saga lies in the depiction of the friendship between Abraham and his God, a friendship with its own intimacies and strains.

Here, again, we find covenant underlining this important relationship. Whereas the covenant at Sinai seems concerned with the response of Israel to the promise of God, the covenant with Abraham emphasises God's commitment to Abraham and to his descendants. Genesis gives us two accounts of the covenant with Abraham, and in the first of these (Gen 15), nothing is asked of Abraham at all. In the other account (Gen 17), the only thing required of Abraham is the circumcision of the males of his household. What is promised in both is a line of descendants for the ancient nomad and a land to call their own.

Stories of the Beginning

The Old Testament was not content with tracing God's involvement back to the beginnings of Israel; it pushes back the horizon of divine activity to the very beginnings of the world. The modern reader must be careful in approaching the narratives in chapters one to eleven of Genesis, for they are written as few other things which we might read today. The larger-than-life characters, the haunting humanity of God, the concern with the origins of everyday realities (legless serpents and rainbows, for example) — all of these are clues that we are dealing with the type of story that scholars call "myth". But take that word out of the mouth of a specialist and put it into normal conversation and it has a nasty sound. Because it can be a particularly useful term, scholars believe that it is worth the effort to bypass the usual connotations of myth and to continue to use it as a description of these chapters.

In this context, then, we need to appreciate what a myth is and what it does. And the first obstacle we meet is our modern fascination with facts. We like our truth wrapped up in neat packages which are tied by mathematical equations, the most recent statistics, documentary evidence and, if possible, the odd footnote. Yet, despite our continuing quest for scientific objectivity in so many fields, we must admit that simple facts cannot deal with the most important thing of all: love and affection, suffering and death, the meaning of life itself.

People have had many ways of approaching these mysteries and of communicating their insights into them; the Old Testament uses one of the oldest and best of these approaches — it tells stories. Far from being the worthless half-lies which are often covered by the term, the real myth embodies some of the most valuable conclusions about life which have been granted to humanity.

We find many of the most familiar Bible stories in these opening pages of Genesis: the creation, the fall, Cain and Abel, Noah and the flood, the tower of Babel. Each of them has its own power to enchant us, its own message to share with us. But when we put them together, as Genesis does, the overwhelming theme is that God created a wonderful world which has been sullied by human sin. Taken as a whole, these stories present us with a type of history of sin to prepare us for the story of salvation which begins with Abraham and continues to Christ and his Church.

Some of the elements of these stories may be factual — there *is* a tower in Babylon, for example — but the stories themselves were never intended to record such petty things as facts when there are greater truths to contemplate. The authors of the early chapters of Genesis did not do their research by looking at the past, but by looking at the world around them. There they saw evil and suffering which they knew to be human intrusions upon God's good plan. These stories describe humanity as a problem which

God created a wonderful world which has been sullied by sin.

God has to solve before they embark on the long saga of that solution.

The Old Testament often gives the impression of being very insular: God has one people, Israel, and he doesn't seem very concerned about anyone else. Here, too, the early stories of Genesis give their own dimension to the rest of the Torah, for they witness to Israel's awareness that Yahweh was the loving creator of all humanity, not just of Israel. As we might expect, the concern of Yahweh with all people is enshrined in a covenant, even in these early pages; it is a covenant with Noah and all his descendants — that is, with all of humanity. Yahweh's concern could not be confined to the boundaries of Israel.

The Sources of the Torah

One question has been lying close beneath the surface of this chapter without quite emerging until now: where do the stories, songs, laws and genealogies which make up the Torah come from? The traditional name attached to the Torah is Moses; he indeed is often its hero and inspiration. In the biblical world a name would often become attached to a book for reasons other than simple authorship; if the book was centred around a figure, for example, or seen as a continuation or re-application of his thought, then eventually that person's name might be found in the title. The ancients were far more nonchalant about authors' names than we are today: most of the biblical books are totally anonymous writings, although some of them have had names attached to them through later tradition.

The material in the Torah came from many different sources, not from any single author's quill. Old stories, told and retold, account for much of it, but here there are differences. Some of the stories were told in the homely sort of settings associated with folklore, others were told in the solemn ritual settings of worship. When we consider that this retelling took place over hundreds of years, we can easily see that the storytellers often put their own imprint on the tradition which had come down to them.

By close study of the texts themselves, scholars have identified four major strands of tradition in the Torah, each with its own way of telling the story and its special concerns. These four major strands are labelled *Yahwist, Elohist, Priestly* and *Deuteronomist,* or J, E, P and D for short. The Yahwist is the master storyteller and oldest of these strands; it calls God by name, Yahweh, and often speaks of him acting and thinking in very human ways. The Elohist is more of a theologian, but also tells stories; it prefers to call the Deity *Elohim* (the normal Hebrew word for God) and has more respect for the distance between God and humanity. The third strand is called Priestly because of its concern with rituals and family trees. The Priestly tradition is quite late (around the time of the Exile and after), and there are signs that people associated with this tradition are responsible for putting the Pentateuch together. The Deuteronomist is mainly to be found in the book of Deuteronomy, although its influence can also be seen in the books from Joshua to Second Kings.

An example of how these sources are to be found in the Torah as we now have it can be found in the very opening pages of Genesis. We are well used to treating the first three chapters of Genesis as one continuous story, the creation and fall. If we look more closly, we might notice that the Deity is referred to as "God" for the first part, and then suddenly — in the second half of Gen 2:4 — as "Yahweh God" (or "LORD God" in many translations). And that is not all that changes. Whereas the first part is solemn and follows a rhythmic pattern (God said ... it happens ... God saw that it was good ... Evening came and morning came), the second part is more relaxed, less structured. Instead of creating with a word, Yahweh moulds man from the dust and builds up woman from a purloined rib. The very attentive reader will eventually notice that the second part is a whole new telling of the story of creation which even has a different order of events (man, animals, woman). It is evidence such as this that led to the discovery of the different strands of tradition.

The first account of creation belongs to the Priestly strand, and is one of the most sublime pieces from that strand. Some of P's concern with ritual can be seen in the description of the sun and moon as celestial markers for the liturgical calendar and the conclusion with the sabbath rest. The Priestly account also calls its creation story a type of family tree: "These are the generations of the heavens and the earth in their creation." (Gen 2:4) Although it is a strange way of putting it (which is why so many translations avoid a literal translation of the verse), it is wholly consistent with another of P's concerns, to construct a genealogy which runs throughout the Torah. When you get bogged down in "so-and-so begat so-and-so", P is usually to blame.

The second creation story, as you might have guessed even from the brief glimpses of the individual strands given so far, belongs to the Yahwist. Who else would think of describing God as getting his hands dirty in creating man, or taking an after-dinner walk in the cool of the evening? What the Yahwist lacks in theological precision, he compensates for with his keen observations on human nature. Examples of that are to be found in the exchanges during the temptation, or in the swift and dexterous passing of blame when the crime is discovered in chapter three.

The beginning reader will hardly be able to discern the separate hands of J, E, P and D at work; yet even the knowledge that they are there (with a few lesser strands as well) helps to answer the questions that arise when inconsistencies are noticed or when a story is recorded twice in different forms. And when a story is *particularly* well told, even the beginning reader might suspect that the Yahwist is at work.

Before leaving the Torah, we must take note of the high regard in which these books are held by Christianity's elder brother, Judaism. The Torah is the beating heart of the Jewish approach to God; its scrolls are still meticulously copied out by hand and are greeted with deep joy in worship. The Feast of Weeks (better known to us as Pentecost) celebrates the giving of Torah to Moses, and the whole life of the devout Jew is an expression of the Torah from morning to night. These books explain to the Jews what they are, but the living out of their principles puts flesh and blood on their special relationship to God. Even though many of the rules and regulations are no longer binding on the Christian, we find much of our identity in these pages as well, both the faith which we have inherited and the attitudes of faith to which we are called. No wonder Jesus insisted that he did not come to destroy Torah, but to bring its principles to their full expression.

The Prayer Life of Israel

TEMPLE, FEASTS AND PSALMS

NOTHING reveals the kind of God we believe in quite as much as the way in which we pray. The person who prays in a perfunctory way with a mind half a mile away from the words might well be imagining God to be a distracted bureaucrat, absent-mindedly rubber-stamping the forms that pass onto his desk. Or is he rather the greedy trader pictured by some people, with their vows and promises of all that they will do in exchange for some special favour? When it comes to drawing unflattering portraits of God by the way in which we approach him in prayer, few are innocent.

Even so, a person could learn quite a bit about Christianity just from the Lord's prayer: that we believe God to be our common Father, that we are awaiting his kingdom, that we look to him for our needs, that forgiveness is central both for ourselves and others and that we can feel helpless in the face of evil and temptation. Likewise, a stranger who came with us when we celebrate the ceremonies of Holy Week would gain many more insights into our faith.

Unfortunately, we cannot attend the great ceremonies of Old Testament worship or watch the solemn rituals. Such has not been possible since the year 70 AD, when the Romans destroyed the Temple in Jerusalem where the liturgy of the Old Testament took place. If our local church were destroyed, it would hardly cause our liturgy to end; we wouldn't be long in trying to build another one to take its place, or, failing that, we would meet elsewhere and continue to celebrate our acts of worship as before, even if it meant less solemnity and convenience. That possibility in itself indicates something of the difference between our churches and the Jerusalem Temple.

The Ark of the Covenant

To understand the Temple, we must go back to a time before it was built, to before the Exodus. The neighbouring nations of Israel all had their own gods, whom they often represented in the form of statues. They believed that the deity would inhabit these statues, and so the idol became for them a real means of the god's presence. There would be times when the god was to be mobilised in battle or was needed to take part in liturgical processions. On these occasions, the statue was carried on a platform by liturgical attendants.

The Old Testament religion — while being quite distinct from its neighbours in many respects — often spoke the same language as the cultures which surrounded it. Yahweh, the God of Israel, was unique in that he was never to be represented in images; so there could never be a cultic image or idol of Yahweh to carry around.[1] But the need for some symbol of Yahweh's localised presence with his people was still felt, and the ark of the covenant filled that need. This ark was a box of wood covered in gold, with poles for carrying, surmounted by two mythical winged creatures, the Cherubim.[2] The ark of the covenant acted as the footstool of

The Romans destroyed the Temple in 70 A.D.

1. Scripture does make some references to attempts to make idols of Yahweh, e.g. Ex 32:1-35; I Kings 12:25-30.
2. A description of the ark can be found in Ex 25:10-22.

the invisible deity of Israel, and like the platforms of the idols, was sometimes carried into battle or borne in solemn procession. The difference was that, on this platform, there was no idol.

The one ark of the covenant gave a certain unity to Israel's worship. It was considered necessary to conduct the national worship only before this ark, in the presence of Yahweh. Of course there were other forms of worship which did not require the presence of the ark, such as private prayer and family rituals; but the central acts of Old Testament liturgy usually took place before the ark.

By its very design, the ark of the covenant was portable. The Old Testament does not give us much of an account of its movements, but it mentions the ark as travelling with the people during the Exodus and conquest of the Promised Land. We also find reference to the ark being lodged in Bethel, Shiloh and Bethshemesh. The impression which the Old Testament gives us is that the location of the ark is of secondary importance; it is the ark itself that matters.

The Jerusalem Temple

But all of that was to change when Israel got a king. When David came to the throne, his first responsibility was to unite the nation behind his rule. He did this by moving the ark of the covenant into his new capital, making Jerusalem the spiritual as well as the political capital of Israel.

It was left to David's son Solomon to build the Temple which was to be the future permanent home of the ark. The Temple and the royal palace stood beside each other as visible proof that Yahweh had chosen the royal line of David to rule over Israel. So we shouldn't be surprised to find that the royal ceremonies are often incorporated into the liturgy of the Temple.

Much of the Old Testament is written by people who would have come to accept that the only place where Yahweh could be properly worshipped was at the Temple in Jerusalem. Even after the ark of the covenant itself was lost forever (in the destruction of Jerusalem in 587 BC) the Temple was thought of as the place where Yahweh dwelt among his people. Naturally, the Old Testament often states that Yahweh cannot be contained by a stone Temple, that his presence there was best explained by saying that his "name" or his "glory" dwelt there. Yet the common Hebrew term for the Temple remained *beth Yahweh,* the house of Yahweh, and it had many of the furnishings of a great person's house, such as candelabras, tables, and burning incense to sweeten the air.

If we imagine the Temple building as a place into which the Israelites would go for their services we are again confusing the Temple with our own experiences of churches. By and large, the liturgies took place outside the Temple building in the surrounding courts. The altar itself stood in front of the Temple, not inside it; and when we consider the large number of sacrifices burnt upon the altar, it is not suprising that the smoke and cinders and blood were kept out in the open air.

Although the Temple building itself would have been a quiet place, the same could hardly be said about the Temple courts. Here were celebrated the great public festivals, the impressive sacrifices and undoubtedly countless private ones also. Here too, various prophets and preachers would teach, and different schools of theology would hold their debates. The gospels point out that Jesus both taught in the Temple courts and argued with his opponents there. Something was always happening on Mount Sion, the Old Testament name for the hill on which the Temple was built.

The Great Festivals

But there were three times of the year in which the activity in the Temple reached its height. These were the feasts of Passover, Pentecost and Tabernacles, sometimes called the pilgrimage feasts, since every adult male in Israel was expected to make the journey up to Jerusalem to join in the celebrations there. And celebrations they were, not unlike our celebration of Christmas with its mixture of religious observance and real enjoyment.

All three of these feasts had an ancient agricultural base, and all three also became overlaid with themes taken from the early history of Israel. Passover, for example, was originally two festivals, Mazzoth (or Unleavened Bread) and Passover itself. Mazzoth was connected with the beginning of the grain harvest, and since leaven was considered a type of impurity, it may have had the overtones of spring cleaning which still characterise its celebration today. Passover, with its slaughter of a yearling lamb, might have originated in a ritual which invoked protection for the flock at the sensitive season of spring lambing. But these feasts have been celebrated for centuries as a combined festival which commemorates the Exodus from Egypt, with the lamb eaten for the long journey's strength and the bread made so quickly that it wasn't given a chance to rise.

The celebration of the Passover Meal still takes place as a highlight of the Jewish year, usually around April. It is so much a family occasion that it seems strange that it should ever have become a pilgrimage feast. But as the paschal lamb became more of an official sacrifice and as sacrifices were only to be offered in Jerusalem, it was inevitable that this family feast came to be centralised in the Jerusalem Temple. Since the Temple is no more, the paschal lamb is no longer the centrepiece of the table, but a meatless shankbone takes its place as a reminder of the more ancient observance. And, of course, when the gospels place the Last Supper and death of Jesus at the time of the Passover festival, all of the overtones of liberation that go with Passover are reapplied to these central events of the Christian story.

The second of the pilgrimage feasts, Pentecost (or the Feast of Weeks), marks the grain harvest. It was celebrated seven weeks after the first sheaf of the harvest had been offered at the combined feast of Mazzoth-Passover. Of the three feasts, Pentecost is the most explicitly agricultural; yet it, too, acquired overtones of Israel's history. It came to be seen as a celebration of the giving of the Torah to Moses, an aspect of Pentecost which is probably reflected in the description in Acts of the Apostles of the Spirit coming upon the disciples on this feast. The implication is that the Spirit of God now replaces the Torah as the guiding force of God's people. Pentecost is the only Old Testament feast to retain its name in the Christian calendar, even though the dates of its Christian and Jewish observances are usually different.

Tabernacles (or Booths) is the most enigmatic of all the pilgrimage feasts. Its characteristic feature (which gives the feast its name) involved the Israelites living in temporary shelters for a week. The custom probably went back to a practice of using temporary huts in the fields during harvest, for this feast was also a harvest festival which had the older name of the Feast of Ingathering. We also know that the celebration of this festival around the time of Christ involved processions and dances and rituals with water and lights; yet the general theme of the festival is a matter of debate.

One theory links Tabernacles with the feast of the New Year and Yom Kippur (the Day of Atonement) in an annual celebration of Yahweh's kingship and of the Temple as his earthly throne. The king would also have had a central role, according to this theory, being renewed as Yahweh's deputy ruler over his people. Yahweh's kingship would be celebrated by a triumphant procession of the ark of the covenant, culminating in a re-enthronement of the ark in the Holy of Holies, the innermost part of the Temple building. The loss of the ark and of the king at the time of the exile would account for the changes in the ritual of this feast. Although this picture of Tabernacles, sometimes referred to as the Enthronement Ceremony or the New Year Festival, fits in well with the evidence of the Book of Psalms and with what we know of the worship of other ancient religions, the matter is far from settled. [3]

For centuries, all of these feasts found a common focus in the Jerusalem Temple. During these festivals the mystery of the rituals, the splendour of music and pomp, the crush of the crowds assembled from all over the Jewish world, and the joy of feasting must have transformed not only the Temple, but the city of Jerusalem itself. The gospels and Acts of the Apostles show that both the Temple and the great festivals had a unique importance to Jesus and the earliest Christians who still participated in the Temple liturgies and observed the feasts of the Jewish calendar. As Christians shared in the wonders of the Temple, so they also shared in the great loss when the Temple was destroyed in 70 AD.

---

3. Mention should also be made of a later feast which was not one of the pilgrimage festivals. The winter festival of Chanukkah is linked neither with agriculture nor with the events of the Exodus. It commemorates the rededication of the Temple after it was defiled by the Greek ruler Antiochus Epiphanes during the second century BC. Chanukkah (or Hanukkah) means dedication; but the festival is also called the Feast of Lights and its celebration involves the lighting of an eight-branched candlestick. Because it occurs in December and involves the exchange of gifts, Chanukkah is often linked with the Christian celebrations of Christmas.

The Songs of the Temple

Yet not everything from the Temple liturgy was lost in that tragedy. The building itself was razed, the furnishings plundered, the sacrifices stopped — but one gem from the Temple survived and has been an ornament of Jewish and Christian worship ever since. The survivor of the Temple and its worship is its hymnal, the Book of Psalms, which has given inspiration to the public and private prayer of the Church since its beginning.

The Book of Psalms, like a modern hymnal, is a collection of materials from different sources and centuries. Like a modern hymnal, it too has many old favourites and a few pieces that no one seems to use. But its most striking resemblance to a hymnal — and the one most quickly forgotten — is that the pieces in it were written to be sung. And if anyone should imagine that the singing of psalms was the sedate (not to mention half-hearted) singing which a modern worshipper can too easily experience, that person should cast an eye over Ps 150, the last psalm in the collection. Among the items mentioned there for the Temple praise of

Psalms were meant to be accompanied by trumpets, harps, flutes, cymbals, drums and dancing.

Yahweh are trumpets, harps, lutes, flutes, cymbals, drums and dancing. Some books of the Bible were undoubtedly meant for reading, but the Book of Psalms was meant for music and celebration!

Of course, all we have of these ancient hymns are the words with the odd clue about how they were performed. Sometimes, the text of a psalm will indicate that it was linked with a procession, as in the case of Ps 68, or indicate an ancient hymn tune to which the psalm was to be sung. There might also be found instructions for the use of instruments, dramatic pauses, gestures and congregational responses.[4] Soloists undoubtedly played their part (just as they do in liturgical music today), especially in announcing the words of Yahweh.

The focus of attention, however, must fall on the lyrics of these ancient songs which, like most lyrics, are moulded into the poetic forms of the culture. Poetry accounts for a surprising amount of the Old Testament: apart from the Book of Psalms, most of the sayings of the prophets and books like Lamentations, Job and Song of Songs come down to us in verse.

If we translated an English poem into Hebrew, much of its poetic quality would evaporate at once; the metre would no longer jangle the words along, alliterations and rhyme would no longer delight the ear, and there would be no play on words to tickle the mind. When we translate a Hebrew poem into English, we also lose the rhythms and word plays, but in an odd sort of way, we keep the rhyme. For ancient Hebrew poetry rhymed ideas rather than syllables.

This rhyming of ideas (which is called *parallelism*) added to a poem's beauty and its impact on the ancient listener. To modern ears, though, it can seem repetitive to the point of boredom, unless the modern hearer becomes aware of how this ancient technique builds the structure and enhances the meaning of biblical poetry. An example or two might help to show how parallelism works in practice.

---

4. Instrumental instructions and directions for silence (the usual interpretation of *Selah*) can be found in Ps 9, although some modern translations omit them. Ps 124:1 tells the congregation to join in, and Ps 134:2 is an example of liturgical gesture.

The first few verses of Ps 54 give an idea of parallelism in one of
its simpler forms:

> God, by your name save me,
> And with your strength defend me.
> God hear my prayer,
> And give ear to the utterances of my mouth.
> Because foreigners have risen against me
> And tyrants look for my life.

Even in these few verses, we can see how parallelism tends to
break Hebrew verse into couplets. Because the example is a simple
one, the first two couplets show how the second half-verse can be
little more than a restatement of the first half-verse in different
words. A modern reader might be excused for thinking that the
third couplet is complaining about two different groups of people,
"foreigners", who have declared themselves the author's enemy,
and "tyrants", who pose a threat to his life. In fact, both of these
terms are describing the same group; like the first two couplets,
the third gives a statement and its echo.

There are other ways in which parallelism can show itself in the
psalms, putting its own stylistic touches onto an individual poem.
The same idea might be repeated in slightly contrasting terms:

> Give ear, God, to my prayer
> And do not hide from my petition (Ps 55:1)

Sometimes the first half-line evokes an image which the second
half-line applies:

> As a father takes pity on his children,
> So Yahweh takes pity on those who revere him. (Ps 103:13)

In other cases, the second half-line extends the thought which the
first half-line expressed instead of simply echoing it:

> Yahweh God has spoken and called the earth
> From the land of sunrise to the land of sunset. (Ps 50:1)

For added effect, a line might have three parts instead of the usual two:

> Shout with joy to Yahweh, all the earth!
> Serve Yahweh with rejoicing!
> Come into his presence with joyful cries. (Ps 100:1)

The careful reader will find parallelism in unexpected biblical places, not just in psalms and prophetical writing, for parallelism represents a whole way of thinking as well as a method of expression. These familiar sayings show how far the effects of parallelism range:

> Do not judge and you will not be judged,
> Do not condemn and you will not be condemned.
> Forgive and you will be forgiven,
> Give and things will be given to you. (Lk 6:37-38)
> The things which are Caesar's give over to Caesar,
> And the things which are God's to God. (Mk 12:17)

Talking of parallelism and the way in which the psalms were once performed may aid an appreciation of their beauty, but it tells us little of what the psalms are about. The simple answer is "Everything!"; there is hardly a matter worth praying about that doesn't have some mention in a psalm. Scholars have broken down this vast collection into categories, and a bird's eye view of some of these classifications will give some idea of the treasures of this ancient hymnal.

Since most of the psalms were used in the Temple, we should expect to find many of them tailor-made to the worship of a large congregation. Hymns of praise, such as Pss 113 and 148, and songs which celebrate Yahweh's kingship, such as Pss 97 or 99, would have found a natural home in these solemn liturgies. In time of great disaster or after a threat had been averted, the Temple worship would have reflected the concerns in everyone's minds; Ps 80 shows the nation beseeching God's help in a communal lament and Ps 124 is an example of a communal thanksgiving.

The king had a special place in many of the Temple ceremonies; his special relationship to Yahweh and to the whole people of

Israel gave the royal office a religious dimension as well as a political one. His kingship is also celebrated in the psalms, possibly remnants from the rite of coronation (Pss 2 and 110). There are prayers for the king (Ps 72), songs of thanksgiving for his victory in battle (Ps 118), and even a special song for his wedding (Ps 45).

But the Temple was a house of prayer for all the people, not just for royal personages. The largest category of all the psalms is the individual lament, showing that people have always tended to turn to prayer when they are in trouble rather than when they're not! Apart from calling God and outlining their troubles in the prayer, these psalms often display a touching confidence in God, sometimes even to the point of thanking him in advance for the help which they expect, as Ps 22 demonstrates. Yet Old Testament people could get just as angry as their New Testament counterparts, and Ps 88 was written by a person who blamed Yahweh for all his troubles. Thanksgiving was also a reason for prayer, even if the frequency of lamentation is greater, and Pss 40 and 107 give us different pictures of worshippers who did not forget God when their prayers were answered.

There are also psalms which reflect on Israel's history (Ps 105), or on the gift of Torah (Ps 119). Some psalms sing of the right way to live (Ps 1) while others try to work out the puzzles of life (Ps 73). While everyone who prays the psalms will be drawn to this or that one in particular, most would agree that the book reaches the heights of spirituality in the psalms of confidence, the songs which centre on the relationship between Yahweh and those who love him (Pss 23,91,121, and 131).

For nearly a thousand years, the God of Israel was worshipped at his temple on Mount Sion in Jerusalem; for nearly two thousand years, the Jerusalem Temple has been little more than a memory. But its songs were never silenced and their strains of praise and petition make the worship once heard in Jerusalem now echo all over the world.

Conflict Between Church and State

THE PROPHETS

T HE person who starts to discuss religion in an open conversation is taking a risk. The person who introduces political topics probably enjoys the thrill of living dangerously. But the one who freely and knowingly raises the question of how religion and politics should be related has definite suicidal tendencies. Anyone who thinks that religion and politics made a more palatable combination in biblical times might read the advice given to Amos when his preaching mixed the two:

> Go, seer. Take yourself off to the land of Judah. Eat your bread there and prophesy there; but don't prophesy here in Bethel ever again for this is the king's sanctuary and a home of the realm. (Amos 7:12-13)

The Prophets in their Society

The Old Testament prophets mixed religion and politics in dangerous quantities, and often paid the price. The popular notion of a prophet as one who gazes into the future doesn't do justice to these great figures. They saw themselves primarily as spokes-persons for God (one way in which the term "prophet" can be translated). They were concerned with what was going on in their own day, not with what was going to happen in the dark and distant future; if they spoke of the future at all, it was generally in the context of the consequences that people's actions would have. Astute observers of the times are still making the same type of predictions today; the Old Testament prophets would have felt far more at home with them than with the modern visionaries whose predictions for the coming year appear in the papers at the end of every December.

Of course, the prophets were not making an innovation when they applied their religious message politically. The whole basis of Israel's existence was to be found in its special relationship to Yahweh, especially as enshrined in the covenant at Sinai. The prophets were only recalling people to the high principles on which their nation was founded and to the God who had given them their freedom, their land and their ideals.

It was a common feature of ancient religions to have great political involvement. The deities, as in the case of Israel, were seen as gods of the nation who were concerned with its prosperity and defence — which is why pantheons are often loaded with gods of war and of fertility. These religions usually took the view: "My country right or wrong", and a major object of their worship was the welfare of the state and especially of the king, often acting as little more than cults of nationalism.

The religion of Israel took a different turn. Although nationalism is an important factor in Israelite worship and thinking, Old Testament religion placed an even greater emphasis on morality. The kings of neighbouring lands may have expected praise and consolation from the spokespersons of their religions, but many of the kings in Israel and Judah felt the whack of a prophet's oracle. In Israel, Yahweh was the ruler to whom even kings were answerable.

Prophecy took many forms in the Old Testament. Some prophets were powerful figures at court, like Samuel and Nathan in the days of Saul and David. Others were holy men without official standing, like Elijah and Elisha. Sometimes they operated in bands whose mobile prayer meetings seem to have provided some amusement for the onlookers.[1] But in the eighth century BC a new development took place. Great prophetic figures arose whose followers recorded their oracles in writing, often adding some biographical material about the prophet and later oracles from the

---

1. Some sense of this amusement still lingers in the story told in I Sam 10:9-13.

Many a king felt the whack of a prophet's oracle.

prophetic followers. These great figures, whose names have become attached to books of prophecy, are often referred to as the writing prophets or the classical prophets.

The books of the prophets might well be called the great theology of the Old Testament. They tease out the meaning of the religion of Israel and apply it in the strongest possible terms to their own day. The prophets refined Yahwism in the forge of experience and produced a vision of faith which was at the same time practical and poetic, a comfort and a challenge.

This should mean that reading the prophets is a stimulating and rewarding experience; unfortunately, for many a first time reader, it is not. Because the prophets were so immersed in their own time and so concerned with what was happening around them, their oracles are often weighed down with references to particular people and events that are lost on the modern reader. Words that would have set the original hearers alight with either sympathetic fervour or heated indignation, now leave modern hearers puzzled. The overall effect can be that of reading the editorial comments from local papers that speak of local issues about which we know little and care less.

As if that weren't bad enough, most of the poetic oracles were written in verse. This undoubtedly helped the disciples of the prophets to remember the prophet's words and added to the effect of the oracles upon the hearers; but it can complicate matters for the modern reader. Plays on words must now be explained in the footnotes or lost altogether, and the richness of the poetic vocabulary can multiply confusion. Just when we feel that we know the meaning of a term like "Israel" (it does mean the Old Testament people, doesn't it?), we find that often in the prophets it refers only to the northern kingdom. We can hardly complain about this, for Israel was the usual name of the northern kingdom; but the prophets also refer to this kingdom by less familiar names — such as "Ephraim", "Joseph" and "Samaria" — often just for poetic effect. And poets in any language can often stretch the language to its limits; the strong imagery that results in the prophets can sometimes be off-putting to us, while the tender images are often lost.

Even the arrangement of the books is a problem. Instead of what we might hope for, prophetic books are often a random collection, not even following a logical (not to mention chronological) order. The state of affairs is even worse than it appears, for the oracles of a prophet's followers can often find their way into a prophetic book, as well as the comments and applications of later editors. While such a process might appear shocking to us, it was the usual way in which works came to be written in ancient Israel. While most of the books we buy and read are the result of one person's planning and composition, most of the Old Testament books were formed through a long process in which many hands and often many generations, were involved. They were not written, in our sense of the word; they *grew*.

If you are getting the impression that reading the prophets requires a bit more effort than some other parts of the Old Testament, you're right. But the effort invested will pay dividends. Naturally, all that this chapter can do is to help you take the first step by looking at a handful of prophets, setting them in their time, and mentioning a few themes from their message.

Amos, the First Classical Prophet
The story of the writing prophets really begins in the northern

kingdom of Israel during the reign of King Jeroboam II (783-743 BC). On the surface, it was a good time for Israel: Jeroboam seemed a strong ruler. Even the author of the second book of Kings — who certainly didn't approve of him — had to admit that Jeroboam did great things for the northern kingdom. Even the length of his forty-year reign stands as a testimony to his competence in those perilous times: Jeroboam's successor lasted only half a year and the man after that only a month. Both were assassinated.

The reign of Jeroboam was marked by military victories. Israel extended its borders as far as the capital of Syria and regained some of the territories which the northern kingdom had lost over the years. At home, affluence reigned, especially in the capital city of Samaria. Many would be tempted to call the reign of Jeroboam the golden age of the northern kingdom.

Amos would have disagreed with that term. Violently. And it must have been very hard for the people around him to see why.

We don't know much about the life of Amos, except that he was a shepherd from the southern kingdom. We don't even know why he moved north. But he settled in Bethel, which was one of the places of worship for the northern kingdom — much in the same way that the Jerusalem Temple was for the southern kingdom. There is even a debate among scholars as to whether he was a qualified prophet or a freelance maverick. In any case, he prophesied in the temple at Bethel, and no one seems to have liked what they heard him say.

Sometimes the translators of the psalms will give them thematic titles, such as "Prayer in a Time of Distress" or "A Hymn for the King's Wedding". If we were to follow their lead, we could entitle the whole of the Book of Amos "Oracles for the Time of Prosperity". The wealth and power of the northern kingdom was not the answer to prayer, as some at the time saw it; it posed the greatest threat to Israel that Amos could imagine. The prophet was not obsessed by ideals of poverty in spirit or of a simple lifestyle; he was consumed by a hunger for *justice*.

Affluence has one major drawback: not everyone can be affluent at once. Where only a few people hold a large portion of society's wealth others will have less than their fair share; the greater the wealth at one end of the scale, the greater the poverty at the other. In our own day, economy is more of a world-wide phenomenon, so that whole nations can live in relative affluence, while the other end of the scale is hidden from view in the Third World; even today, someone has to pay the price of our wealth.

So the message of Amos was at base a cry for justice. He denounces the wealthy who have so spoiled themselves that they have become blind to the suffering around them. He highlights the afflictions of the poor victims of ruthless business tactics. He satirises the boredom of those whose only goal in life is pleasure.

But most of all, Amos looks around at his society and says that it just can't last; the nation will fall, the people will be deported, and the history of the northern kingdom will come to an end. It must have sounded like rambling rantings to an audience in the reign of Jeroboam. Just when the nation was back on its feet, when the standard of living was up and Israel was at the height of its military strength, trust a prophet to go around trying to make people feel insecure!

One of Amos' greatest grounds for complaint was the religious life of Israel. Falling numbers of worshippers and poorly conducted ceremonies were not the problem; Amos was angered that the elaborate liturgies at Bethel were completely unrelated to morality in the daily life of the people. The very people who could

The message from Amos must have sounded like rambling rantings.

crush the less fortunate for the sake of a few silver coins saw no inconsistency between their merciless attitudes and their worship of Yahweh.

> I have come to hate and despise your feasts,
> And I will take no pleasure in your assemblies.
> For if you bring me whole burnt offerings and sacrifices of grain,
> I will not accept them,
> And the peace offering of your fattened beasts I will not receive.
> Get the noise of your songs away from me;
> I won't listen to the music of your harps!
> Let justice go forth like water instead.
> And let righteousness be an ever-flowing river. (Amos 5:21-24)

When Amos threatened the people with the end of their nation, he was not simply broadcasting gloom or speaking on behalf of an angry God. He realised that the basis of Israel's nationhood lay in the demands of its religion; when these were weakened — especially in terms of social justice — Amos recognised that Israel's very fabric was beginning to unravel. His message was a warning and an invitation: return to God could still avert the dreadful future.

Broken-hearted Hosea

Hosea also prophesied during the reign of Jeroboam, a little after Amos. His book contains some of the most powerful, sensitive, shocking and enticing pieces to be found in all of the prophetic writings. He gained valuable new insights into the relationship between God and his people through the experience of his own broken heart.

During this time, the worship of Baal was common in the northern kingdom. Baal was a fertility god, responsible for the produce of the land and the herds, and his cult involved the devotees having sexual relations with prostitutes attached to Baal's shrine. Hosea's wife was involved in this type of cultic prostitution.

Since this type of action is so distant from our experience, many today find it very difficult to sympathise with Hosea's plight. Yet

Hosea loved his adulterous wife; even after the marriage had broken down, he made attempts to win her back, always hoping that she would come to love him as he loved her. And at some stage it struck him: his own love of an unfaithful woman was like Yahweh's love of unfaithful Israel in pale reflection; his agonised frustration was teaching him about the longing of God for the love of his people. As Hosea discovered what a marriage should not be, he was discovering what the covenant should be: not shallow, meaningless sacrifices but a deep commitment from Israel to cling to their God.

Hosea also warned that the Israel that he saw could not survive for long, and he — even more than Amos — could watch the clouds forming and the storm beginning to rage. The superpower of Assyria was beginning to gain strength and to turn its attention towards the regions in which Israel lay. The leaders of Israel tried every strategy, at times asserting their independence, at times playing up to Assyria, at times making overtures to the other superpower, Egypt. After the king of Israel withheld the annual tribute money (in less lofty circles, we would call it protection money), the Assyrian armies moved in and eventually the capital of Israel fell in 722 BC, less than twenty-five years after the end of Jeroboam's prosperous reign.

Isaiah the Hopeful

At about the same time the most famous of all the classical prophets arose in the southern kingdom of Judah. Isaiah was more of an optimist than Amos or Hosea; he delighted in the promises of Yahweh to his people, and during these turbulent times, the promises kept Isaiah's heart high.

Especially important to Isaiah was the promise to King David that his descendants would always reign on his throne and that through them, great blessings would come to Israel. But things were little better in Judah than they were in the northern kingdom; the ruling classes were accumulating land, leaving many homeless and without a means of livelihood. One king at this time, Ahaz, was a particular disappointment. His international politicking compromised the pure religion of Judah and eventually led to the destruction of the northern kingdom. Ahaz's personal religion also left much to be desired: he sacrificed his son to pagan gods.

Even an Ahaz could not deter Isaiah's hope. Isaiah was not slow to denounce the injustices of his own day, as his brother prophets were doing in Israel; but he also spoke of a king to come who would be the fulfilment of everything that God wanted in a king. Even though Isaiah was probably content that these oracles were fulfilled in the great king Hezekiah, whom Isaiah lived to see, his oracles were later interpreted in light of the Messiah whom God would send as the perfect son of David.

The Book of Isaiah is especially complex, for the school of thought which followed his outlook continued on for more than two centuries. Their oracles are also included in the book which bears Isaiah's name. An important example is the collection of oracles which make up chapters forty to fifty-five, often referred to as Second Isaiah or Deutero-Isaiah (both these terms mean the same thing). This collection dates from the time after the fall of Jerusalem at the beginning of the sixth century BC while the people were in Babylon, the period known as the Exile. This time of desolation and exposure to another culture with its strange ways and its strange gods proved to be a very fruitful time for the theology of the Old Testament. Second Isaiah, for instance, is one of the first to show that Yahweh is not just the only God for Israel, he is the only God for all humanity. That realisation would later stand behind the early Christian movement to go beyond the boundaries of God's Old Testament people and to bring the gospel to those who had been pagans.

It would be hard to overstate the contribution of the writing prophets. In their writings we discover hard realities, such as the emptiness of a religion that doesn't spill over into life, or the meaning of justice. The prophets share with us their new insights into God: the tenderness of his love, his concern for all humanity, the strength of his expectations, the consolation of his promises. They were people who believed that God had something vital to say to their time, and delivered their message with courage. They were often rejected and persecuted for their pains, but most often they complained that they were shouting into deaf ears. People who believe in the relevance of God to the affairs of their time are the descendants of the prophets in every age.

Life and its Problems

Wisdom

YOUR life can be transformed by a visit to the local bookshop: you can discover there the secret to fitness through a new diet, or ten new rules which will remodel your ability to think. The key to success in business, systems to break the bank at the casino, methods to hammer your obviously inadequate personality into a social dynamo are all packaged away between paper covers for your convenience. The American humorist, James Thurber, probably had the best idea of all in the title of his response to the self-help books of his generation, *Let Your Mind Alone!*

Despite the present flood on the market, some self-help books are worthwhile. They can contain sound advice, useful hints, valuable insights, and shed new light on the problems which beset us. That would certainly be true of a whole group of books to be found in the Old Testament.

These Old Testament books are usually called the "wisdom literature" and they represent the closest thing that Israel had to philosophy. Philosophy through the ages has often meant an exploration into the speculative and metaphysical, touching questions such as the reality of material being, the existence of God, the certainty of knowledge, the nature of the soul; the wisdom literature in Scripture would hardly qualify as philosophy in these exalted and sublime terms. Wisdom was much more down to earth for the Hebrew; it simply meant finding the best way to live.

Proverbs and Sirach
The books of Proverbs and Sirach (or Ecclesiasticus, as some

bibles call it) are full of this type of practical advice, framed in short sayings which capture the lessons of experience in a few phrases.

A dish of greens where there is love is better
than stall-fed beef when hatred comes with it. (Prov 15:17)

Wealth keeps adding many friends
while the poor person is isolated from his neighbours.
(Prov 19:4)

These sayings can also be longer, presenting a whole picture for our consideration. This portrait is painted with touches of humour to drive its point home:

"Who says 'Oooh'? Who cries 'Woe'?
Who has fights, who complains, who has wounds for no
 reason?
The person who delays over wine,
The one who goes to try wine mixed with spices.
Do not gaze at wine when its red grows deeper,
When it sparkles in the cup and goes down smoothly.
Afterwards it will bite like a serpent,
Like a poisonous snake it will sting.
Your eyes will see mirages,
Your mind will tell you lies.
You will be like a person who tries to sleep at sea,
Who lies down on a tottering masthead.
'They hit me, but I didn't suffer;
They must have beat me, but I didn't know it.
How long till I get up?
I need another drink.' (Prov 23:29-35)

Proverbs are still with us, of course, bits of advice summed up in a handful of words. Often enough when we quote them in everyday conversation, we will find ourselves introducing them with a phrase such as "Great-aunt Matilda always told me 'Never trust a

How long till I get up . . . I need another drink.

man who dyes his beard.' " And much of the Old Testament
wisdom probably has its roots in these living observations and rules
of life that are handed down from generation to generation, which
is why they are often framed as advice given from a father to his
son:

My son, do not forget my advice.
Your heart must guard my commands,
For they will give you length of days,
A doubled lifespan, and peace. (Prov 3:1-2)

But as well as this folksy sort of wisdom, these books are
influenced by the thinking of other nations. Some of the proverbs
found in the Old Testament are reflections of proverbs which we
also find in Egypt and Mesopotamia. And because much of the
wisdom literature is tied into this international wisdom tradition,
some of the wisdom books have little of that concern with God's
action in the history of Israel that characterises so much of the Old
Testament in general.

We might well ask how this international wisdom found its way
into Israel. The answer is to be found in the royal court: as wisdom
taught the individual to govern his own life, so it was the virtue of
rulers, showing them how to govern the affairs of state. Every
court had its specialists in wisdom, its sages and advisors, who
knew how to evaluate a situation and the best course of action to
take. There is much in the Old Testament wisdom which reflects

the lives and concerns of these higher civil servants, telling them how to behave in the presence of powerful rulers, how to conduct themselves at royal banquets, advising them to steer clear of revolutionary plots, as well as guidance for the ruler:

> When a ruler listens to things that are false,
> All his attendants will be mischievous.
> When a king gives true justice to the poor,
> His throne is established forever. (Prov 29:12,14)

The Old Testament had no doubt who was the wisest man who ever lived. It had to be Solomon, for the proof of his wisdom was to be found in the security and prosperity of Israel during his rule. Quite apart from this vision of wisdom as a royal virtue, Solomon opened up the frontiers of Israel through international treaties and the importation of foreign advisers. During his reign, Israel was probably exposed to the international wisdom tradition as never before.

One of the more poetic developments of wisdom thought in Israel is the portrayal of wisdom as the companion of God. If wisdom was the virtue of kings, then it must belong to the great ruler of all in a special way. Lady Wisdom sings her praises in Prov 8 and Sir 24, describing herself as being with God before creation itself and playing a part in the ordering of the universe. In Sir 24, Wisdom goes on to say how she made her home in the midst of God's people to invite them all to taste of her treasures. When the hymn which begins the Gospel of John is compared to these two chapters, several echoes can be heard, for the New Testament saw that Wisdom really entered the human world in the person of Christ.

Sometimes modern readers will be so struck with the practical, workaday approach of writings like Proverbs and Sirach that they wonder how they were ever thought of as religious. Indeed, much of the thought contained in the wisdom literature is quite secular, concerned with getting on in life. But to the ancient Israelite, this was a religious concern. Since they had no idea of afterlife, they were convinced that God rewarded virtue in this life. If you were good to God, he was good to you, and among his blessings would be prosperity, a large happy family, and many years to enjoy it all.

This outlook is known as *the theory of divine retribution:* God uses the experiences of everyday life to reward the good and to punish the wicked. According to this theory sickness, accidents and misery were always due to the sins a person had committed; the sinner would watch in agony as the just person went from strength to strength.

On one level, the theory of divine retribution makes perfect sense. To the believer, God is in control of everything. If that is true, doesn't it follow that he sends to us both the good things in life and the bad? And why would he give us sorrow and suffering except as punishment for our sins? The theory of retribution might sound simplistic and naïve, but believers restate it anew today every time they exclaim: "What did I do to deserve this!"

Of course it wasn't always the virtuous and God-fearing who rose to the top of the heap in Old Testament times any more than today. And it wasn't always the wicked who had catastrophe fall on them from the blue. The traditional outlook couldn't last forever, but pulling it down was no easy job.

Qoheleth the Disillusioned

The attack on the theory of divine retribution came from within the wisdom tradition, the same tradition which had relied on this theory for so long. The Books of Qoheleth (or Ecclesiastes) and Job are the two main prongs of the biblical attack on this outlook, and both are considered literary gems of the Hebrew Bible.

Like most Old Testament books, neither Qoheleth nor Job is the product of one person's quill. Qoheleth (not really the author's name, but a title meaning "one who addresses the assembly") laces his reflections with sayings from the older wisdom tradition, sometimes contrasting them with one another, sometimes contradicting them with his own observations. Because Qoheleth seems so negative, at times a later hand has added a more pious note, with the result that there are three streams of thought in the book as we now have it.

The end of the book identifies Qoheleth as a sage, a teacher in the wisdom tradition; but for the purposes of this book, he indulges in a literary fiction and takes on the role of King Solomon.

This not only had the advantage of putting these observations in the mouth of the wisest man who ever lived, but it also enabled Qoheleth to speak as one who had received all the blessings of wealth and pleasure that God was supposed to give as the reward for goodness. At first this type of attribution seems slightly dishonest and misleading; it was no more deceptive to the original audience than a speech put into the mouth of an historical figure by a modern playwright is to us today.

Qoheleth's opening observation has earned its place in English phraseology as the great summary of disillusionment:

Vanity of vanity, says Qoheleth.
Vanity of vanity, everything is vanity. (Qoh 1:2)

He complains that he has tried every pleasure and accumulated great wealth, but nothing has satisfied him. He even tried the study of wisdom until he became wiser than anyone who had ever lived, but it failed to bring him happiness. The problem was death: how can life have any meaning or any lasting enjoyment as long as death stands as the great brick wall which a person can never cross. So Qoheleth found the theory of divine retribution wanting; even if God did give the good person all the blessings of life, the key to happiness was not to be found among them. Death ended all life's pleasures and the thought of death could turn enjoyment sour.

Qoheleth also noted that goodness did not always bring even this unsatisfactory reward. Since life is unpredictable and reward is uncertain, Qoheleth advises his audience to forget about dreams and live in the present. His positive message is to enjoy what you do here and now — not because of what it might or might not bring you in the future — and to appreciate God's gifts as they come.

Job, Suffering and God

The Book of Job also delivers a crushing blow to traditional wisdom thinking, even more directly aimed at the theory of divine retribution. Its development was even more complex than that of the Book of Qoheleth, probably spanning many centuries in its composition.

It began life as a folktale about a hero named Job. Job was the model of virtue, and — as the theory of divine retribution would expect — he was amply blessed for his troubles with a happy family and great wealth. Then Job's world collapsed: tragedy destroyed his wealth and killed his children; a second wave of misfortune even took his health away until we find Job sitting on a tip head, scratching his boils with bits of broken pottery. But Job prays to God, who listens and restores all Job's wealth, and even gives him more children and a ripe old age.

This part of the book is written in prose and follows a pattern which we know of from other ancient writings. In those other stories, the calamity has struck because the hero has committed some sin which he didn't even notice. When he told his deity that he was sorry and begged forgiveness, everything was restored as the theory of divine retribution demanded. But there is no "secret sin" involved in Job's downfall. In fact, the whole point of the story is that sinless Job can suffer like the rest of us.

Nearly as famous as Job himself are his three friends, "Job's comforters". They aren't much comfort, though they try to do the

Job's comforters weren't much comfort.

best they know how. Every one of them seems to have been a charter member of the "Theory of Retribution Fan Club". They tell Job that if he confesses some small sin that he overlooked before, life will be rosy again; Job insists that there is no such sin. They speak with passion and poetry of the justice of God and of God's great goodness; Job accuses God of being his tormentor without cause. Getting a bit fed up, the friends say that Job is too wicked and stupid to understand God's ways; Job protests that neither the friends nor God himself seem to have much understanding of the problems of living life on a tip head. The speeches in Job are a place where the wisdom literature really tries to wrestle with the basic problems of life; maybe the problems win, but at least the reader feels that it was an honest fight.

In the course of his arguments, Job appeals again and again to the divine tribunal. He seems to feel that the hardest thing of all to take is the silence of God in the midst of his suffering. At the end of the book, God appears and gives two speeches which point to the marvels of creation as proof of his wisdom. Yahweh never tries to explain to Job what has happened or why it has happened; he merely points out to Job that there is little place for human questioning of divine actions. The experience of God finally satisfies Job when arguments did not. As he acknowledges God's mysterious wisdom, he says:

My ears had heard tell of you,
But now my eyes have seen you.
Because of this, I am ashamed.
I comfort myself for being dust and ashes. (Job 42:5-6)

The book doesn't end there, however. The real sting in the tail of the tale is that Job's three friends, the ones who felt that they knew all about God and how to defend him against Job's attacks, were the ones in need of forgiveness. Yahweh tells them that they were the liars and blasphemers, not Job, even though what they said sounded so pious and reverent. It must have been quite a shock to the many early readers who would have identified with the theological positions of Job's friends.

If the exodus from Egypt was the liberation of Israel, the Book of Job was the liberation of Yahweh. It freed him from acting according to human standards, allowing him to soar above human justice and human wisdom. Even though the theory of divine retribution had found occasional hiding places in the Old Testament writings, the Book of Job evicted it from biblical thought. Only God knows and fully understands God's actions; wisdom belongs to him alone.

Qoheleth and Job shine like stars among the books of the Old Testament; they have an attraction for many thinkers and authors whose interests do not lie chiefly in the realms of theology. Carl Jung's "Answer to Job", Robert Frost's "A Masque of Reason", and Archibald MacLeish's play *J.B.* all bear witness to the fascination that Job still arouses, just as Peter Shaffer's *Equus* pays tribute to the power of its language. These two books can stand on their own in any company, either as provocative theology or as masterpieces of the writer's craft.

Yet when we place them in the stream of biblical thought, we find that their contribution is basically a negative one. The old thinking was too pat and had too many of the answers. Job and Qoheleth were needed to restore the mystery to life and to acknowledge the depths of such problems as death, suffering and the silence of God. These two books cleared the theological site of its congested growth: as well as the mighty oak of divine retribution, the thorny bushes of pious platitudes and false religious security were all levelled by this double-headed axe.

A New Solution: The Book of Wisdom

But Job and Qoheleth created a problem of their own: if the righteous can suffer, if virtue need not be rewarded in the world of our experience, where is God's justice? Both of these books still imply that God is just in his dealings with humanity, though the ways of his justice are unknowable. People might be able to dig down into the earth and make the rocks yield their treasures, says the wisdom poem of Job 28, but they will never discover how to mine wisdom:

God alone understands the way to wisdom,
He alone knows its home. (Job 28:23)

It was this vacuum in the vindication of Yahweh's justice that opened the way for one of the greatest advances in biblical thought, one so important that we take it for granted in our religious thinking today.

This development appears briefly once or twice in the later writings of the Old Testament, but its most eloquent presentation is in the first part of the Book of Wisdom. After Wisdom describes the thinking of the godless who trouble the life of the righteous, the book continues to show how and where their philosophy went wrong:

> Such were their thoughts, and they were deceived.
> For their own wickedness blinded them,
> And they did not know the mysteries of God,
> Nor did they hope for the reward of piety,
> Nor consider the prize in store for spotless souls.
>
> Yes, God created humanity for immortality,
> Even made him an image of his very own likeness.
> Through the devil's envy death came into the world;
> Those of his party will discover what it is.
>
> But the souls of the just are in God's hand,
> And torment will never touch them.
> In the eyes of the foolish, they seemed to die,
> And their leaving is seen as oppression,
> And their journey from us as destruction.
> Yet they are at peace.
> Even though in human reckoning they seem punished,
> Their hope is filled with immortality. (Wis 2:21-3:4)

Once Wisdom had grasped that life for the virtuous does not end at death, she could sweep away all of the lingering fragments of the theory of divine retribution: The childless person can still reap the reward of faithfulness when the envied children of wicked people bring them sorrow. An early death need not be the sign of divine disapproval; it might be God's gathering of human fruit when it is ripe with virtue. Evil people may seem to get away with murder and live comfortable lives, but they will know nothing of the rewards that God has in store for the just.

The resurrection thinking of the Book of Wisdom brings us right to the threshold of the New Testament. It was not only written in the same language, Greek, instead of the more usual Old Testament Hebrew, but also shows considerable signs that it had come to terms with the thinking of the Greek world which was also to make its imprint on the pages of the New Testament. After our journey through centuries of Old Testament thought and writings, it is only a short step of a few decades from the Book of Wisdom into the world of early Christianity.

From Palestine to Rome

NEW TESTAMENT SETTING AND HISTORY

IF you have felt lost at sea at times during our voyage through the Old Testament you will be relieved to learn that we have reached the sandy shores of the New Testament and its world. Any modern reader will feel more at home here where we know many of the stories and where some of the characters seem like old friends. For most Christians, opening the New Testament after an excursion into the Old will seem like a homecoming.

But our familiarity with the first century world does not often run very deep. Since its history, its various cultures and its politics are so important to the New Testament writings, we will spend a bit of time renewing and deepening our acquaintance with the era from which the New Testament comes.

First century civilisation seemed to wrap itself around the Mediterranean Sea; world power had moved west from the ancient powers of Egypt and Mesopotamia to settle with the world-conquering race of the Romans. Rome excelled in such things as armies and administration, which not only allowed it to expand its sphere of influence to nearly any place where it was useful to do so, but also to give a new civil order to the areas under its rule.

Gods and Emperors

Even though Rome had been around for some time, it had recently undergone drastic changes in its own structure. Its traditional rule by representative legislators had been largely replaced by the person of the emperor. The first century witnessed an impressive parade of emperors, from the respected and respectable Augustus down — with a definite emphasis on "down". Gaius Caligula, for

Caligula afraid of Jupiter's counterattack.

instance, reigned as emperor for four years, gripping the influential classes in Rome with the terror of unpredictable bloodshed. To exercise his divinity (he seemed quite convinced that he was a god), he declared war on Jupiter, the chief god of the Roman pantheon; but then he would hide under his bed during lightning storms, afraid that Jupiter was launching a celestial counter-attack. Nero, who was to have quite an influence on early Christian history, was more concerned that people appreciated his human talents, performing for audiences in both sports and the arts; appreciation was compulsory. Nero's madness (not just his bad poetry and atrocious singing) made him one of the most hated of all emperors. Even after his death, some Romans were afraid that he was really still alive (in Parthia, not Brazil) and would yet regain control of the Empire. Towards the close of the century, Domitian insisted on widespread worship of the emperor under the title "Lord and God"; traditionally, his reign was one of persecution for Christians, though the evidence for this is scant.

By the year of Domitian's death in 96 AD the books of the New Testament would have the same form in which we know them today, though the decision as to which books belong in that select list was still generations away.

Rome may have had the administration, but Greece still ruled the culture. It was not the pure Greek culture of Plato and Sophocles, but the hybrid culture that was the legacy of Alexander's long dead empire. The common language of the Roman world was not Latin, but Greek, which even made its way into Rome itself. The popular philosophies of the day, Stoicism and Epicureanism, were both descendants of Greek outlooks. No wonder that the common designation of the age is "Hellenistic", an adjective which means "Greek-ish".

Palestine was also affected by the Hellenistic culture of the

The Romans were afraid that Nero was still alive after his death.

Roman Empire, though to a lesser extent than other lands. For the early missionaries, the spread of the gospel meant coming face-to-face with this culture and learning to speak its thought forms in a meaningful way.

Of course, the largest obstacle to the gospel in the Hellenistic world was the wide variety of religions afoot. The most prominent of these were the state cults, involving worship of the major deities of Rome. In the eastern provinces of the empire, worship of the goddess Roma and of the guardian spirit of the emperor (which evolved into worship of the emperor himself) formed an important part of the state religion.

The state cult had very little to do with the individual person, except in his capacity as a member of the state. Naturally people wanted something more than that, and they often became devotees of one of the unofficial religions. Most of these were characterised by ecstacy and great secrecy, or perhaps the initate would be made privy to knowledge or an experience of the deity which would be his or her sure sign of salvation. Some of these private cults are referred to as mystery religions, and there are grounds for thinking that they were even greater rivals to Christianity than the state cult.

Magic and superstition also raged in the Roman world. Fate was an even stronger notion in most people's minds than were the gods: the Etruscans who lived in north-central Italy, for instance, had an oracle that they would come to an end as a people during the century now under our consideration. When the time came, the Etruscans seemed simply to give up hope and disappeared as a culture; though other factors were obviously at work, many historians feel that the Etruscan reverence for their destiny was among the major reasons that they vanished as an identifiable culture. Magic and superstitions, notably astrology, were attempts to influence a cosmos which was beyond control. In marked contrast to this, Christianity brought importance to human choice and freedom; according to the gospel, even though circumstances may remain often unpredictable and uncontrollable, the ultimate destiny of a person depends totally on the decisions that person makes. This outlook was probably not at least of Christianity's attractions in the fatalistic Roman world.

The Homeland of the Gospel

Palestine was a corner of the Roman Empire which was slightly different from the rest. Other peoples accepted Roman ways and religion with relative ease, but the strict Jewish worship of one God made this an impossibility in Judaea. Hellenism and the Greek language made their inroads, but not to the same extent as elsewhere around the Mediterranean Sea. Then, too, the Jews held on to their national aspirations when other subjugated nations seemed quite content to let the Romans hold the reins of power.

Palestine itself was a land of complexities, more so than the modern reader of the gospels usually thinks. Its different regions all have their own tale to tell: Galilee, the homeland of Jesus, had a mixed population of Jews and pagans; the Galilean Jew was held in slight suspicion by his Jerusalem counterpart, thought to be lax in certain aspects of keeping the Law and sloppy in his pronunciation of liturgical Hebrew. Peraea, too, which lay to the east of the Jordan, had a mixed population of Jew and pagan. The Decapolis region (the name means "Ten Cities", though the number of cities varied) was founded after the Roman conquest of Palestine; this league of city states was entirely Hellenistic with a pagan population. According to the gospels, Jesus had followers from the Decapolis region and exercised his ministry there, though not as much as in Galilee. Samaria also features in the gospel accounts. The population there was the result of the fall of the northern kingdom in the eighth century BC and intermarriage between the Israelites and the pagan settlers. Although the Samaritans worshipped the God of the Old Testament, their worship was looked upon as a corrupt abomination by the Jews; hatred between the two races went both ways — its track can be seen in the parable of the Good Samaritan and even more clearly in John's story of the Samaritan woman at the well.[1] Tyre and Sidon are also mentioned in the New Testament, but they never formed part of the lands of the Old Testament people; they belonged to the lands of the Phoenicians and their thoroughly pagan background is assumed by the gospels.

1. The parable of the Good Samaritan is in Lk 10:25-37, and the story of the woman at the well in Jn 4:1-42.

Palestine During the Life of Jesus

Of all the regions of Palestine, Judaea held the pride of place for the Jew. Within its boundaries lay the great city of Jerusalem and the Temple of Yahweh. The name itself is a Hellenised form of the name of the southern kingdom of Judah. This region was so prominent that foreigners applied its name to all the descendants of the Old Testament people, no matter where they came from or from which tribe they were descended; to the outsider they were all "Judaeans", the Greek word for Jew.[2]

The figure which predominates in the political arena of first century Palestine is undoubtedly Herod the Great. In many ways, he was a pitiful, paranoid figure, pathetically playing up to any Roman faction if it would help retain his own power, and slaughtering members of his own family when they seemed to become rivals to his throne. This led Augustus Caesar to remark in a rare witticism that he would rather be Herod's pig than Herod's son — Herod, being a nominal adherent of Judaism, would not have dreamt of eating pork and so his pig would be safe — but he seems to have had few qualms of conscience about assassinating his sons.

For all his faults, King Herod was a great builder. In the New Testament his most remembered accomplishment was the restoration of the Temple, so extensive that some look upon it as nearly being a new construction. The visitor to Jerusalem today would seldom think of omitting to visit the Western Wall, or "Wailing Wall" as it was once known; this was only a supporting wall for the platform of Herod's Temple area, yet there are few who would remain unimpressed by the masonry. Herod also built or improved several fortresses, the most famous of which was Masada near the Dead Sea.

Since Herod the Great died in 4 BC, the name in the gospels usually refers to his son Herod Antipas who ruled Galilee (and not the whole of his father's territory). He was never given the title of king by the Roman overlords; when he went to Rome to petition for this favour, his enemy Agrippa sent charges against him so that, instead of returning to Galilee as king, Antipas ended up as an exile in Gaul.

2. This probably still leads to confusion in our translations today. John's Gospel, for instance, has the reputation of not liking the Jews, whereas it is quite likely that it doesn't like the Judaean Jews who seem somewhat stricter than other Jews.

Judaea itself was governed by a Roman procurator, responsible directly to the emperor. The procurator normally resided at the Hellenistic city of Caesarea on the Mediterranean coast, a place more congenial to the Roman way of life than the overtly Jewish city of Jerusalem. Jewish and Christian sources agree that Pontius Pilate, the holder of this office from 26-36 AD, was a person of cynical arrogance, though we know little about him from other sources.

The Priests

Religion and politics were as interwined in first century Judaea as they had been in Old Testament Israel, which meant that Rome's power was tempered by the power of the religious establishment. The Jerusalem priesthood, unlike modern systems of religious leadership, was a matter of heredity rather than choice; until the second century BC, this hereditary system even extended to the office of the high priest. After the return from exile, the high priesthood began more and more to take the place of the king in the restored province. By the dawn of the first century, Herod had already taken it upon himself to depose high priests and to replace them with his own appointments, an example which the Romans were glad to follow. Thus, in the gospel accounts of the passion of Jesus, two men are referred to as high priest: Caiaphas (the current holder of the office), and his father-in-law Annas (who had been deposed, but who retained the high priestly dignity).

In addition to the high priest himself, there are others who are sometimes referred to as "the chief priests". These would be holders of special offices, such as Captain of the Temple (a priestly rather than a military designation), or leaders of the different teams of priests who served in the Temple liturgy in rotation. These priestly dignitaries were to be seen in quite a different light from the usual members of the priesthood: while the leaders of the priesthood seem to have been a wealthy and influential class who could turn their religious position to considerable personal gain, the usual son of Aaron lived in the provinces and only served in the Temple one week out of every twenty-four.[3] The power and

3. Such was the situation of Zechariah, the father of John the Baptist, according to Lk 1:8-9

affluence was concentrated in the Jerusalem priesthood; the provincial priest was comparatively impoverished and powerless.

Sadducees and Pharisees

The leading members of the priesthood belonged to the religious party known as the Sadducees. Their theology was minimal and conservative: they acknowledged only the Torah as the inspired Word of God and refused to believe doctrines such as the resurrection which were not contained therein. Their rivals were the Pharisees, a religious party composed of laymen, to which most of the scribes (experts in Torah) belonged. The Pharisees held the respect of the people of their day, known as they were for their care in keeping the Law as exactly as they could. Their knowledge of the Law was so thorough that even the Sadducee chief priests, who were no friends of theirs, would turn to them for advice on how to carry out the Temple worship according to the Torah.

These two great parties came together in the Sanhedrin, the great council which met in the Temple complex in Jerusalem. The Sanhedrin functioned as a court, as we see from the New Testament, and was composed of both the leaders of the priests and the great experts in the Law — in other words, Sadducees and Pharisees respectively. The seventy-one members of this great council represented the highest native authority in Judaea, although the exact extent of their power is uncertain.

The Essenes

There were other religious parties active in Palestine in the first century. The party of the Essenes has come to prominence recently because of the discovery of the Dead Sea scrolls near what appears to have been an Essene monastery in Qumran. Their highly organised community life and strict observance of the rules of ritual purity, together with their commitment to celibacy, communal ownership of property and absolute obedience to their superiors remind us of Christian monastic orders, but the Qumran community had a warlike attitude which is alien to our usual notions of monastic ideals. They looked forward to the day when God's people would engage in a decisive battle with the enemies of

God, the battle between the Children of Light and the Children of Darkness. The Qumran community disappeared during the period of the war with Rome, possibly as a result of their participation in that religious and political struggle. Apart from this monastery near the Dead Sea, other Essenes lived a more secular life; one ancient source says that they were to be found in all the cities and major towns of the region.

The Zealots

The Zealots formed another movement on the Palestinian stage. They were political freedom fighters against the Roman occupation forces and against Roman sympathisers, but their political terrorism had a strong religious base. For them, the first commandment to honour Yahweh alone meant that no foreign power could be tolerated as overlord of God's people. Their religious observance was so strict in matters of the sabbath and ritual purity that some consider them to have been an extremist splinter group from the Pharisee party. The Zealots had their end and their most glorious hour at Masada where they resisted a Roman siege for years; when it became apparent that the Romans were about to breach their defences, the defenders of Masada committed mass suicide rather than surrender to the conquering army.

The People of the Land

The vast majority of people were not affiliated to any of these groupings. They were referred to, at least by the Pharisees, as the "people of the land" (*'am ha'arez* in Hebrew) and were thought to be dangerously lax in their observance of the Law and ignorant of its precepts. A Pharisee was forbidden to buy produce from one of these people, for fear that the proper tithes had not been paid on the crop — one indication of the extent of the divisions caused by these religious parties of the first century. Most of the followers of Jesus and his sympathisers would have come from "the people of the land", although there are indications in the New Testament that members of the other parties might also have been among his disciples.

Acts of the Apostles

For the early history of the Christian movement on this Roman and Palestinian stage, we are largely dependent on the New Testament itself, especially the work we call Acts of the Apostles. That book is not really an account of the activities of all the apostles; its concern is more to show how the Christian gospel was brought from Jerusalem to the capital of the world from where it was certain to spread to all of humanity. The title of this chapter comes from this plan and vision of early church history in the book of Acts. Our brief glance at New Testament history will follow the broad outline of Acts of the Apostles.

After the resurrection and ascension of Jesus, Luke (the author of Acts) shows us the church as a community living in Jerusalem. There they proclaimed Jesus as Messiah to all who would listen to their message.

The modern Christian might be struck by their lack of missionary activity outside Jerusalem itself, but this should not really be seen as very surprising. The Messiah was, after all, for the Jews, a fulfilment of the Old Testament promises made to Israel, not to all of humanity. So it made sense to be based in Jerusalem, the capital of Judaism, where the good news of Jesus could be preached most effectively to the greatest number of God's people. Of course if this situation had been allowed to continue, Christianity would have remained a movement among Jews, which would have left most of us outside the picture altogether.

The Hellenists

Among those attracted to the message of the gospel were those referred to in Acts as the "Hellenists". All over the known world there were settlements of Jews (sometimes called the "Diaspora" or the "Dispersion"), some dating back as far as the sixth century BC. For these Jews, Jerusalem retained its central importance, although they were often influenced by the places where they lived. Sometimes their contact with paganism would make them more tenacious of their traditions; sometimes it would make them re-evaluate what was central to their religion and what was only secondary. Since the preaching of Jesus had also engaged in this type of re-evaluation, it was only natural that it should appeal to some of those Jews, once members of the Diaspora, who were now settled back in Jerusalem; these are the Hellenists of Acts.

Stephen was the most prominent member of this group, and apparently a very powerful speaker. His radical outlook landed him before the Sanhedrin where he was accused of preaching against the Temple. Indeed, his speech as we find it in Acts may be difficult for a modern reader to follow, but it left the Sanhedrin audience in no doubt as to its message: Stephen was preaching that God did not need the Temple, and that the authorities connected with the Temple had proved themselves religious failures by the crucifixion of Jesus. Stephen's fine oratory made him the first Christian martyr.

After the death of Stephen, a few years after the death of Jesus, the Hellenists had to leave Jerusalem because suspicion concerning their religious orthodoxy had been aroused. Interestingly enough, the Twelve (who were not Hellenists) were able to remain in the city without danger when the Hellenists were fleeing to the outlying districts of Judaea and Samaria.

Being in danger did not stop the Hellenists from proclaiming the message of Jesus wherever they went, but this caused problems since they were not only in Jewish territory but also in the towns of the hated Samaritans. There would have been a number of the early Christians who felt that the Messiah was only for proper Israelites, not for these half-breed Samaritans who were only half-Israelites. So when the Hellenists (in the person of Philip) took the revolutionary step of accepting Samaritans as Christians through baptism, the Holy Spirit did not come upon them! Then Philip sent to the apostles in Jerusalem who sent Peter and John to Samaria. When the apostles laid hands on the Samaritans, they received the Holy Spirit just as the Jewish converts had before them. This incident is usually remembered because Simon Magus tries to buy the power of bestowing the Spirit, or even because some see in it an early reference to the sacrament of confirmation; its real importance in Acts of the Apostles is that people who were not Jews according to the norms of the times were received into the church for the first time with the approval of the apostles.

Conversion of the Gentiles

The next step was to bring in those who were not members of God's people at all; the pagans or, as most translations of the Bible call them, the Gentiles. Acts presents this picture in three stages. The first shows Philip the Hellenist baptising an Ethiopian eunuch who is obviously a devotee of the Jewish faith, but who could never fully become a member of that faith community. Philip decided to go ahead and receive him as a Christian anyway. These Hellenists seem to have been an impetuous bunch!

The second stage in the reception of the Gentiles has a more official flavour: Peter, as leader of the Twelve, is sent to baptise Cornelius, a Roman centurion. Peter's reluctance to take the step can be seen in the triple vision he had telling him to call nothing ritually unclean that God has declared clean; after this vision, messengers from Cornelius arrive and Peter goes with them. While he is preaching the good news of Jesus to Cornelius, the Holy Spirit comes upon Cornelius and his household, and Peter rightly takes this as a sign that he should delay no longer in accepting these Gentiles into the church through baptism.

By and large the pagans involved were already sympathetic to the religious ideas of Judaism. Many Gentiles accepted the idea of one God, which lay at the heart of the Jewish faith, and its high moral ideals; nonetheless, there were certain stumbling blocks which prevented these people from becoming full converts to Judaism, notably the dietary laws and the practice of circumcision. While some Gentiles did become full converts to Judaism (or proselytes), a larger number accepted their beliefs and certain of their practices (such as the keeping of the sabbath) and were sometimes called "God-fearers". It was primarily these God-fearers (who formed only a small minority of the Gentile population) to whom the apostles Barnabas and Paul turned their efforts.

This was such a dramatic step that it was certain to receive dramatic opposition. The objection was that the Messiah was meant for Israel, not for the pagans; if these pagans wanted to benefit from the Messiah, let them become Jews first. The matter was decided by a general meeting of the apostles and other leaders of the church in Jerusalem. The decision was to let the pagans become members of the church, making only the demands which would have been expected of them as God-fearers; it was a great victory for Paul and Barnabas, and it is the centrepiece of the whole book of Acts.

Acts of the Apostles continues to watch the spread of the gospel throughout the life of Paul as he brings the good news to new audiences such as the philosophers of Athens (who reject it by and large) and the Roman colonists of Corinth (who unexpectedly give it a hearing). Paul's ministry led him back to Jerusalem where he was arrested and from where he was eventually sent for trial to the emperor's court in Rome. Luke ends his picture here, with Paul under arrest, yet freely preaching the gospel in the capital of the world, around the year 61 AD.

Persecution

We are able to carry the story a little farther than Acts, even though we sadly miss Luke's help in doing so. We could sense in Acts that the opposition of the Judaean religious establishment to Christianity was growing; but we should also remember that the early Jewish Christians still saw themselves as devout Jews, Christianity being for them a new development in their religion rather than a new religion. The Jewish Christians continued to observe the Torah, albeit in the new spirit which Jesus showed, and to frequent the Jerusalem Temple. The leader of the Jewish Christians was James, the Brother of the Lord,[4] who appears more than once in Acts. James seems to have been prominent enough to be the pawn in a power play by the Jerusalem priesthood; during an interregnum between Roman procurators, the priestly authorities showed their strength by putting James, the Brother of the Lord, to death, which indicates that Christianity was still acting as a major irritant to the Judaean authorities.

More devasting persecution was to come from another quarter. In Rome — as elsewhere — converts to Christianity came from different social backgrounds, but especially from the bottom rungs of society's ladder. Their close-knit communities, half-Jewish

---

4. The term "Brother of the Lord" has been understood since ancient times to refer to James (and others) as a member of the extended family of Jesus, either a cousin or a foster-brother.

ways and exotic sounding beliefs coupled with their undesirable social status made them a natural target for suspicion. So when the city of Rome was burnt in a massive fire, the emperor Nero blamed the Christians for the tragedy. The common opinion of the time was that Nero started the fire himself to clear a site for his ambitious building projects, in which case a scapegoat was urgently needed.

The resulting persecution lasted from 64 to 67 AD. Roman Christians were executed in a variety of ways, for by this time the Romans had made death into a macabre art form. Some were put to death for the entertainment of Nero's guests in his private circus on the Vatican hill; the tradition that St Peter met his death here and was buried nearby accounts for the basilica named for him on that hill today. Tradition also dates the death of St Paul during this trying period.

In Palestine, matters were also coming to a head. The religious nationalism of Israel finally erupted into revolt in 66 AD, provoked by the arrogance of a particularly inept procurator. But the Jews were no match for the superpower of Rome, and in 70 AD Jerusalem fell and the Temple was destroyed, never to be reconstructed.

The destruction of the Temple had profound effects on Judaism and also on Christianity. That the House of Yahweh should be destroyed by pagan conquerers meant a profound crisis of faith for Judaism, one which the parties of the Sadducees and the Essenes did not survive. It became more urgent to draw the boundaries between those who were Jews and those who weren't and it was soon decided that Christians fell outside the boundary. That in turn must have caused trauma to many Jewish Christians who considered themselves not only followers of Jesus, but devout Jews.

In effect, the destruction of the Jerusalem Temple brings us to a natural stopping point in the history of the early church, for it brought about the sharp division between Jew and Christian. That division was coming for a long time, both because of the opposition which Christianity received from the Judaean establishment and because of the influx of Gentiles into the ranks of Christians. The truth of the matter is that the Christianity which we meet in the New Testament, while deeply rooted in the religion and the language of the Old Testament, has already broken its nationalistic bonds. It is no longer a denomination within Judaism, but a faith open to people from every race and backround. The remaining nineteen centuries of church history are only an extended footnote to that development.

The Four-Dimensional Portrait

THE GOSPELS

IT may have seemed strange to begin the section on the New Testament with snatches taken from Acts of the Apostles rather than a discussion of the four gospels. After all, the gospels not only appear at the beginning of the New Testament but describe events that took place well before the events in Acts.

The explanation for this approach is simple: In our days of world-wide wire services and televised on-the-spot reporting, it is easy to reach the wrong conclusions about the gospels. We nearly imagine the evangelists (or authors of the gospels) following Jesus around, recording every word and making notes on every encounter, and writing it up as quickly as possible afterwards as if to meet a newspaper deadline. As a result, we often think of the gospel stories as simple reports of events "the way they happened" — and the less the evangelist colours the way that his stories are told, the better we feel that he is at his job.

The truth is that the gospels were not written until more than thirty years after the death of Jesus. All of the events recounted in the last chapter had taken place before the last of the gospels had taken its final form, and most of them before the first evangelist put quill to papyrus. Before we can appreciate the gospels for what they are, we have to remember the many crises and challenges that Christianity had met in the intervening years, and try to reconstruct how the sayings and deeds of Jesus played their part in the life of the early church.

The twentieth-century person naturally questions why the gospels were not written sooner. The simple answer is that writing something down was not as casual an affair in the first century as it

The Evangelists were not like modern journalists.

is today. The expense of writing materials and their unsatisfactory performance would have made the modern pen and paper seem like a miracle (without even mentioning the electric typewriter or the word processor). Then, too, we usually think of writing as an aid to our memory; in fact, it is a way to forget. The telephonist who scribbles down a phone message, the professional who makes a note of an appointment in a diary, the student who writes furiously during a lecture — all of these are excusing their memories from the onerous task of retaining information by putting it in writing to which they can refer again when the need arises. The words and deeds of Jesus did not need to be written at first, for they formed the *living* memory of the early Christian community.

The Writing of the Gospels
One of the earliest references to the writing of the gospels comes from the first half of the second century; the source is the bishop

Papias who prided himself on trying to trace all of the traditions about Jesus to their earliest sources. He quotes one of these when he says:

> The elder also said this: Mark had become Peter's interpreter and wrote down accurately as much as he could remember of what the Lord said and did, but not in proper order. For Mark neither heard nor followed the Lord himself (during his earthly ministry), but was later a disciple of Peter's, as I said; and Peter adapted his teachings to the needs of his audience without trying to make an orderly account of the Lord's sayings.

Scholars differ on how accurate a picture Papias presents us with, for he himself is writing half a century after the events it refers to.

Still, Papias was alive during the time when the gospels were being composed, even if he didn't witness their manufacture, and his is the oldest description of the process that we have. Without putting total faith in the details of Papias' account, we can discern a few points on which both Papias and modern scholarship agree:

1. *The gospels as we have them come from people who were not themselves eyewitnesses to the life of Jesus.* Although we are familar with the gospels under the names of the individuals Matthew, Mark, Luke and John, none of the gospels claims such authorship for itself; these names all became attached to the gospels through later tradition. Papias clearly presents us with a picture of a gospel which is written by someone who is not an eyewitness and who relies on the reports of others.

2. *The traditions which are incorporated into the gospels have been influenced by the needs of the community.* Papias notes that Peter had already adapted his material to the audience he was addressing. The most obvious way in which this affected the tradition was in selection: if the whole Gospel of Mark is read aloud, it would only take about an hour and a half to complete the exercise. The amount of material which must have been omitted from the public ministry of Jesus is phenomenal; the stories and sayings which remain are there because they met certain needs in the community. Other methods were also employed, such as telling

the story in a way that emphasised a certain point or linking together sayings of Jesus to bring out the common theme. The gospel traditions were not just concerned with reporting words and events, but with communicating them in a way that was meaningful to the Christian community.

3. *The gospel writers themselves put a personal stamp on the traditions which had come down to them.* Papias is careful to note Mark's faithfulness to his tradition; yet Papias himself records the important information that the order in which things appear in Mark's Gospel belongs, not to the older traditions, but to Mark himself. This may not seem of overwhelming significance to the modern reader until it is realised that this structuring and arranging of material in Mark's Gospel is the key to understanding Mark's message. The influence of the individual evangelists can be seen more clearly when their accounts of the same teaching or happening are compared, for their characteristic concerns can often be seen in the different ways in which they present the same material.

Before the composition of the gospels in our Bible, the material was preserved in a number of ways. Papias mentions the use of the raw material of the gospel as part of the teaching of Peter. We might think that the main business of early teaching was to tell the story of Jesus; but if we take the New Testament letters as an indication of the major concerns of early Christian catechesis (for most of them predate the gospels), we find little of the life of Jesus in them. Rather, the message of these letters centres on our relationship with God the Father, the new life which Christians are called to lead and the salvation won for us by Christ.

In other words, in its initial stages a phrase like "the Good News (or Gospel) of Christ" did not so much mean "the Good News about Christ' as "the Good News brought by Christ". This can be seen clearly by looking at the teaching of Jesus in Mark or Matthew; very little of his teaching is about himself, but rather about God the Father and the life he expects his disciples to lead. So these isolated stories and sayings would have been used chiefly as material to illustrate and substantiate the points of a teaching session.

But some stories were undoubtedly the point itself. Again, turning to the New Testament letters for evidence, we see that the death and resurrection of Jesus are at the heart of the earliest Christian teaching. Some form of the passion account was probably the first lengthy narrative to take shape along definite lines as a connected story, not just as a story but perhaps as part of the liturgy of the early Christians; there would be little doubt that the story of the Last Supper would be handed down through its use in Christian worship, so possibly the same is true of other parts of the gospel tradition.

There were probably other compositions which had their effect on the four gospels in circulation before the gospels were written. We usually forget that the Old Testament was not available as a handy one-volume collection; the complete Old Testament came only in the form of expensive and cumbersome scrolls. Therefore a convenient series of texts which pointed to Jesus and to his life, death and resurrection was probably drawn up for the use of Christian teachers. We have such a compendium of texts from the Old Testament among the Dead Sea scrolls, though it is naturally related to Essene beliefs rather than Christian beliefs, and Papias credits the apostle Matthew with compiling a series of "oracles of the Lord" which might conceivably fit this description.[1]

Another pre-gospel writing possibly in circulation in the first century, but now lost to us, is a compilation of the Lord's teachings with a minimum of narrative about his life. The words of Jesus have had a fascination for Christians greater than that of any other part of Scripture. Elaborate editions of modern bibles sometimes have the words of Jesus printed in red type to distinguish them as especially important; this is no innovation, for some ancient manuscripts had already employed different coloured inks to separate the words of Jesus from the rest of the gospel. There is evidence for the existence of such a list of sayings in those passages which are present in both Matthew and Luke though missing in Mark. Many scholars feel that these can be accounted for by a compilation of sayings (referred to as "The Q

1. This suggestion is only speculation, for the phrase which Papias uses is too vague to interpret with precision. It is due to this statement of Papias that the first gospel is attributed to St Matthew, though the likelihood of an apostle having written this gospel is almost nil.

Document'') which was available to the author of these two gospels but unknown to Mark. Though the existence of such a document remains outside the realm of proof, its availability to Matthew and Luke would explain the relationship between the first three gospels so well that most students of the New Testament accept its existence with few qualms.

Why Write a Gospel?

Now that we have some picture of how the raw material of the gospels circulated during those thirty-five to forty years between the death of Jesus and the writing of the first gospel, we are in the position to ask what motivated the first evangelist to put his gospel together; if the church had got along well enough without a written gospel up to this point, why did it not continue along those lines?

One reason has already been hinted at: I referred earlier to writing as excusing the memory; perhaps it would be truer to say that in the ancient world what was in danger of being forgotten was written down. Due to factors as diverse as persecution and simple old age, the sixties marked a time when the eyewitnesses to Jesus were beginning to die; with the realisation that the second coming might not be as imminent as some had thought, it was seen as imperative that the traditions about Jesus be preserved at this stage.

There was also a need for a clarification of what Christians believed. The early church was no more immune from heresies and bizarre theologies in the first century than it would be in later centuries; perhaps it was even more susceptible to them in these formative years. On the one hand, conservative Jewish Christian elements still pressed the harsher demands of the Torah on Gentile converts. On the other hand, some Gentile Christians happily blended esoteric pagan beliefs with their new faith. By setting down an account of the life and teachings of Jesus, the evangelists were clarifying what was basic to Christianity by "going back to the roots", as it were.

There was also a growing awareness that the figure of Jesus himself was at the heart of the Good News which Christians were proclaiming: the "Good News of Christ" was shifting its meaning from the "Good News brought by Christ" towards the "Good News about Christ". The new insights into the meaning of Jesus would find their expression in the form of the written gospel account. To begin appreciating the four gospels means to see that they are works of theology — and often very sophisticated theology — rather than simple biographies.

Since each of the gospels presents a continuous story of the life of Christ, the distinction between a gospel and a biography isn't always apparent at first glance. Let's take an example: while browsing through a collection of old books, I run across one with the title *A Life of Frederick Kickturn, Master of the Dancing Camels.* Because I have a twin interest in choreography and animal training, I sit down and read the biography. It doesn't matter that I have never met Frederick Kickturn nor that I am unlikely to hear of him again. The book begins with his humble birth, proceeds through his unsung career, and ends with the tragedy of his death. When finished, the book is returned to its place on the shelf without having had a major effect on my life. Now contrast that with the reading of a gospel: The gospel, too, proceeds through the life of Jesus toward his death; but instead of ending there, goes on to the resurrection.

And therein lies the difference, for the risen life of Jesus means that I am reading about a person with whom I can enter into a deep relationship of faith; and faith is the real purpose of the gospel, the real need for which these four documents are written. In the words of the clearest declaration of intent to be found in the gospels themselves:

> Now Jesus did many other signs in the presence of his disciples which have not been written down in this book. These signs, though, have been written so that you may believe that Jesus is the Messiah, the Son of God, and so that, as believer, you might have life in his name. (Jn 20:30-31)

If the gospels were simply biographies, it would make little sense to have four of them in the New Testament; it would be far better to sift through their evidence and blend together what is found in them as best as possible. Indeed, people have done this since ancient times, and very elaborate modern editions of the four gospels woven into a continuous narrative are still to be had. But something vital is lost in the process.

The four gospels represent four different approaches to the person of Jesus, four different representations of his mission and his meaning, four distinct theologies of Christ. Each picture is carefully constructed by the way stories and teachings are hung together, by the choice of material to be included or excluded, by the telling of an incident with the emphasis on a certain part. As soon as we start blending the theologies of the evangelists, we end up with a muddle. The best approach to a gospel is to read it and to absorb it without reference to the other three. Only after each gospel has been seen on its own should all four be put together mentally to bring out the full richness of the gospel portrait.

Mark's Patterned Picture

Mark's Gospel shows clearly how the arrangement of a gospel helps to frame its message. At a casual glance, there would be little in Mark's Gospel to startle the modern reader: the stories and sayings are familiar, not least of all because they are heavily used in two of the other gospels. If you are the type of reader who skips through material until you reach something new, you may find that you have only thumbed through Mark's Gospel instead of reading it. The Christian who is used to getting Scripture in small doses (as in the readings at the Eucharist) may not even notice that in a document such as a gospel these same doses are connected; the individual incidents may still be appearing to him as the small doses that he is used to.

When Mark's Gospel stops being a collection of small doses and is seen as one continuous story, strange things happen. The Gospel breaks into two halves, with marked differences. In the first half, no one knows who Jesus is, except the demons and he won't let them speak; in the second half, he begins teaching his disciples about himself. In the first half, the disciples are clearly on Jesus' side; in the second half, they often disappoint him, misunderstand him, and eventually betray and deny him. In the first half, the emphasis is more on healings and miracles; in the second half, the emphasis is on the teaching of Jesus and the demands of being his follower. The first half seems to extend the invitation of Jesus; the second half gives the message of the cross. And the centrepiece of it all is the confession of Peter, "You are the Messiah" (Mk 8:29).

Mark uses the arrangement of his material to great effect. The careful reader will notice that, even though Mark lets his audience in on the secret of Jesus in the very first verse, all the figures in the gospel have to discover who Jesus is.

And when Peter announces the conclusion of the disciples, that Jesus is the Messiah, the secret isn't really known, for the disciples still think that perhaps the Messiah is all about wealth and success and political power. Jesus has to teach them that the Messiah is about suffering and rejection and death before God's Kingdom can come. The Gospel of Mark seems at times stern and stark, its language is often sparse, even awkward; yet it effectively paints a portrait of Jesus and his mission which can have great impact. It also seems to be the first of the gospels to have been composed, breaking ground for a whole new way in which to express the Christian vision.

Those who wrote after Mark elaborated the gospel form, making it more literary and sometimes more theological; perhaps that accounts for the popularity of Matthew and Luke over Mark through the centuries. But the gospels of Matthew and Luke both owe much of their material to Mark (as well as to the Q Document mentioned before); and so these first three documents are usually grouped together and referred to collectively as the "synoptic gospels", a term which implies that they share a common point of view on the life of Jesus.

Since they are more complex works than the Gospel of Mark (and the Gospel of Mark has its complexities too), Luke and Matthew are impossible to summarise. All that can be given here are a few pointers to their vast treasures.

Luke — A Gentle Gospel
It is generally agreed that Luke is a gospel for Gentiles, even that Luke is one of the few non-Jewish writers in the New Testament. Perhaps being a Gentile in a movement which was so Jewish in its origins has made Luke more sensitive to people who would have been less acceptable in first century society; his gospel is filled

with characters that are less than respectable, such as the tax-collector, the sinner, and the Samaritan. Because women were given such an inferior status in the Palestinian way of life, Luke is at pains to show the accepting attitude of Jesus towards them, his sympathy with their problems, and their help to him in his ministry.

We might be amazed that this Gentile gospel has as much concern with the Old Testament as any of the other three; this seems to indicate that the early Gentile Christian had a greater appreciation of the Old Testament scriptures than does his modern counterpart. Many of these early converts would have belonged to the group known as God-fearers, and the Hebrew scriptures (in their Greek version) would have been their Bible. In fact, one of the most important pictures of Jesus which is presented by Luke is that his life is the key to understanding the Old Testament, especially through the death and resurrection. Since Jewish missionaries were presenting the Hebrew scriptures as a complete revelation of God, it was important for Luke to show that these ancient books needed to be brought to completion through the life and teaching of Jesus. The stories of Christ's birth and childhood which are found in the early chapters of Luke are composed in such a way that it is clear that even the coming of Jesus fulfils much Old Testament hope and promise.

One of the finest aspects of Luke's portrait of Jesus would have been especially attractive to his Hellenistic readers: the teacher who trains his disciples into his vision. In modern language, teacher is not quite the term, for it may conjure up one whose activity lies mainly in the classroom; the type of teacher which Luke has in mind would correspond more closely to what is known as a "guru", though without the negative overtones which the term sometimes carries today. Jesus was a teacher who taught, not only by what he said, but by the example he gave in everything he did. Those who wanted to learn from him at the deepest level did not stop at listening to what he had to say; they travelled with him, sharing his life, learning from their every experience with him. The major section of Luke's gospel relates the story of the journey from Galilee to Jerusalem (Lk 9:51-19:28), framing the image of Jesus as the teacher and the Twelve as his closest disciples.

But every reader of Luke's Gospel is also meant to join in this learning experience with the Twelve, and the gospel spells out solidly the facts about what the life of discipleship entails. The Holy Spirit appears again and again in Luke, for the gift of the Spirit is what makes discipleship possible. We are told that disciples must be keenly aware of forgiveness, both the forgiveness which God the Father has given them, and the forgiveness which they must show to those who offend them. And the danger of riches, which can turn the human heart from God, is stressed again and again.

Luke lays a special stress on other themes which are to be found in Mark and Matthew, bringing them to new prominence. We not only find teaching about prayer in Luke's account, but many pictures of Jesus himself at prayer. Luke's Gospel also contains the three great canticles used daily in the prayer of the Church: the *Magnificat,* the *Benedictus* and the *Nunc Dimittis.* Prayer and praise punctuate Luke's Gospel, never letting the reader forget the role of God the Father in the drama of the Christ event. And often in this prayer, we find the note of joy which also tints many of the scenes which Luke depicts.

Jerusalem gives a natural focus to the geography of all four of the gospels, both because it was the religious and political capital of Palestine for the Jews and because it was the site for the events of Good Friday and Easter Sunday. Luke brings out this importance by making the whole centre section of his narrative the journey to Jerusalem, as mentioned before. He also begins and ends his gospel in that city, more precisely in the Jerusalem Temple; by doing this, Luke is setting the stage for his second book, Acts of the Apostles, which will bring the gospel from God's Old Testament city to the peoples of the world until the Good News of Jesus reaches Rome, the capital of the empire. Luke's Gospel is the only one of the four to continue the story of the Good News from the life of Jesus to the story of the early church by means of a second volume.

Matthew — A Gospel for the Church

We generally refer to the first gospel which appears in the New Testament as the Gospel of Matthew, but there are good reasons for saying that the apostle Matthew was not the author; his name became attached to the first gospel because of an ancient tradition that Matthew drew up an account of the Lord's oracles in the language of the Hebrews, and since this first gospel is clearly the most Jewish, the tradition of Matthean authorship came to rest on it quite early. But this gospel is thoroughly a product of someone working in the Greek language, not a translation from Hebrew or Aramaic; so if the ancient tradition was accurate in saying that Matthew wrote something in a Semitic language, it was not intending to speak of this first gospel. If Matthew did produce a document, it was either incorporated into the gospels of the New Testament as a source or it is now lost to us completely.

Another good indication that the first gospel in the New Testament was not the work of one of the Twelve is its heavy dependence on sources, not only for its material, but for its structuring of the story of Jesus. Although the Gospel of Matthew is the first to appear in the biblical table of contents, it was not the first to be written; that honour goes to the Gospel of Mark, as has already been indicated. The Gospel of Matthew uses this earlier gospel, as well as the Q Document and other sources that seem to have been available to this evangelist alone; dependence on sources, which themselves were not eyewitness accounts, to this extent is hardly likely if the Gospel of Matthew were the composition of an eyewitness, as the apostle Matthew would have been.

What we can say about the author of Matthew's Gospel depends on the evidence of the document itself. It obviously comes from a Jewish Christian setting and is meant to speak to Jewish Christians, although most scholars would take the fact that it was written in Greek as evidence that it was written outside Palestine, perhaps in Syrian Antioch where there was a sizeable community of Jewish Christians. The gospel shows considerable ease with rabbinical methods of approaching Scripture together with a highly developed theological outlook, leading many commentators to think that the evangelist was someone who had trained as a scribe before becoming a Christian. The community for which Matthew's Gospel was written still maintained a respect for the Jewish Law, living it according to the new light shed on it

Matthew knows that the Christian community is not without its faults.

by the teachings of Jesus. Unlike some of the extremists, the author of Matthew's Gospel and his community knew that Jesus is Messiah for Gentiles as well as Jews; these Jewish Christians had come to terms with the sad fact that many of their own people would never accept the Messiah who was sent for them first and foremost. The Jewish background of the author and of his community gives this gospel insights into Jesus which are grown in the same Old Testament soil from which Jesus' own actions and teachings sprung. For the sake of convenience, we continue to call the author of this first gospel Matthew, even though we do not mean the apostle of this name.

Matthew's Gospel is perhaps the most orderly of the four. An outstanding feature is the skeleton of five major discourses around which the gospel is built, perhaps in imitation of the five books of the Torah. Certainly, Matthew tries to show us that Jesus is the New Moses, giving the new law of God and establishing the new covenant. Even more important to Matthew is to show Jesus as the promised Son of David, a title that the Gospel of Matthew uses of Jesus twice as often as the rest of the New Testament put together. The promise to David guaranteed that David's line would continue to rule God's people throughout the ages; the great formulation of this promise also said of David's son, "I will be his father, and he will be my son." (2 Sam 7:14). Matthew takes this promise and develops it according to his faith in Jesus as the divine Son of God.

If Jesus is the sure fulfilment of God's promise in Matthew's Gospel, then the Twelve are the authentic continuation of the message of Jesus. The community of faith is our point of contact with the living Christ in Matthew's vision, and it is only in his gospel that the word "church" actually appears. Matthew knows that the Christian community is not without its faults, and he is not above showing them through the shortcomings of the Twelve; yet he sees the community of believers as the means through which the Good News of Jesus will take effect in the world of humanity. For this reason, Matthew's Gospel is sometimes singled out as that which best shows the place of the church as still speaking and acting in Jesus' name.

The Unique Gospel of John

John's Gospel obviously stands in a different tradition to these three synoptic gospels. Whereas the first three gospels are packed with sayings and actions, John concentrates on a handful of incidents and explores each of them for its depth of meaning. Even the way the speech of Jesus is reported in this gospel is peculiar to John. Whereas most of the ministry in the synoptics takes place in Galilee, much of the activity in John occurs in Jerusalem; whereas the public ministry of Jesus in the synoptics could fit into the span of a single year, the dates indicated in John would demand two or three years. The synoptic gospels spin their separate theologies of Jesus from much the same sort of yarn, but John is using sources which seem on the whole to be available to him alone.

The authorship of this fourth gospel has been one of the burning questions of New Testament study for many years. Even though there is much to be said in favour of the tradition which connects this gospel with the apostle John, the gospel in its present form comes to us in a second or third edition, reworked by someone other than the original author. A quick glance at the last two chapters of John provides one bit of evidence in this direction: the end of chapter twenty gives a neat, graceful conclusion to the work, but chapter twenty-one is then added, partly to comment on the death of the disciple upon whom the gospel relies. There are other signs of a later editor's hand here and there in the gospel; so even if we identify the disciple whose testimony lies behind the gospel as the apostle John, as I myself am inclined to do, we must acknowledge the influence of other hands in giving the final shape to the book.

Questions of authorship hold their own fascination, but they only shed a limited amount of light on the message of the gospels themselves. John's Gospel has one basic consideration, the person and work of Jesus and its significance. We find no great body of moral teaching in John to match Matthew's Sermon on the Mount. Even the parable stories, with their lessons of forgiveness and perseverance in prayer and working for the Kingdom of God, are notable by their absence. The only burning moral issue in John's Gospel is the decision to believe in Jesus or to reject him; all else, even the love of one another which is so prominent in John, follows from this.

The realisation that the Good News brought by Jesus is to be found in the person of Jesus himself reaches its height in John. His gospel shows that Jesus is the complete gift of God to humanity, the bread by which we must live, the giver of living water to quench our thirst, the vinestock from which we draw our very life. We are trained to discover the relationship of Jesus to his Father, a relationship of complete obedience and dependence, so that we can model our relationship to Christ in the same mould.

John uses language which connects the incidents in his narrative with the liturgical life of the Christian community. Water, bread, fruit of the vine and even anointing are all to be found in John's Gospel, indicators that the same Jesus who was once at work in Palestine is now at work in the life of the church. Yet, for John the real proof that Christ is alive and among his followers lies in the love and unity which they try to build among themselves, a special type of love which is only fulfilled when they have loved each other as Jesus has loved them.

John's Gospel probably embraces the longest time span between the events it records and the final form of its account. We should see these years as a period of deep reflection during which the words and actions of Jesus came into focus, especially in light of the experiences and crises of the early communities. More importantly, the meaning of Jesus himself was becoming clearer as the years progressed; it took these decades to scale the theological heights which the fourth gospel reaches, and it was worth the wait.

If these few pages have seemed to stress how distinct the four gospels are in their portrayal of Jesus, then it is time to say that it is indeed the one figure which emerges from these four different corners. As in a good piece of choral music, each of these voices might have its own melody, but they blend beautifully together to make one overwhelming assault on the human spirit. Each of the four narratives is wonderfully distinct, each of their theologies unique, yet all four are doors which open into the same room.

No, the gospels are not biographies about some remote figure of the past; they are documents about a living person who can transform our lives. They are even channels through which the living Jesus makes his voice heard in our ears, shines his light for our eyes, and touches our hearts with the warmth of his love; and biography is too small a word for all of that.

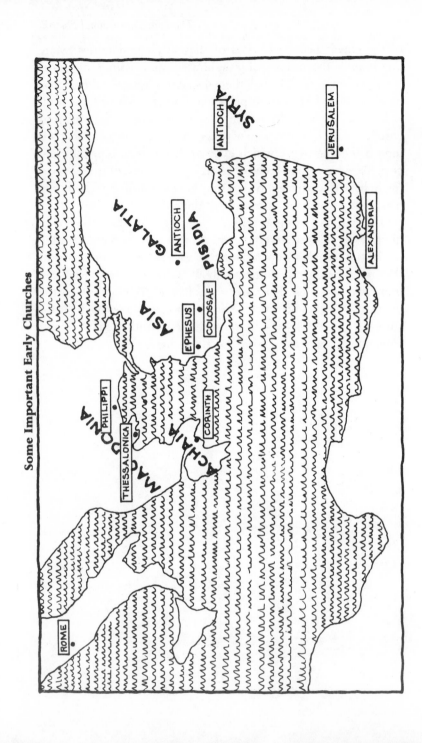

Some Important Early Churches

Tentmaker and Theologian

ST PAUL

THERE aren't many people whose letters have made a lasting impact on the world. The odd letter to the editor may have its influence, and correspondence received from fiancé — or revenue commissioner, for that matter — may make all the difference to the person who receives it. But letters tend to be ephemeral items: opened, read, and destined for the obscurity of the filing cabinet or the bin.

The great exception was St Paul; the thought contained in his letters has influenced Christianity more than any other single factor, with the exception of the person of Jesus himself. Nearly half of the books in the New Testament are in the form of letters which purport to come from Paul's hand.

And the vast majority of them really are letters; that is, they are addressed to people that Paul knows, prompted by specific situations which have arisen, buried up to the gills in the current affairs of the local community. Paul's theology was not the result of academic research, published in learned journals; naturally there was considerable study and reflection behind Paul's thinking, but the fuse which ignited it was the experience he had as a missionary and as a pastor. If it were not for the problems he met and the difficulties of his communities, Paul's massive input into Christian thinking might never have been made.

Background information is always helpful in interpreting any piece of writing; but in the case of Paul's letters, it becomes doubly important. His revolutionary impact on early Christianity can only be appreciated against the backdrop of his personal struggles and conquests; his message can only be evaluated by looking at the situations and communities for which it has been tailored. Our sources for this information are basically to be found in the Acts of the Apostles and the letters themselves; what follows here is an overview of the pictures from these sources.

Paul originally had the good Jewish name of Saul; but he was not born a Palestinian Jew. He hailed from the city of Tarsus in Asia Minor (present day Turkey). As a Jew of the Diaspora, he would have had a certain acquaintance with Hellenistic culture and non-Jewish ways of thought; his origins also supplied him with Roman citizenship, a much prized possession in the first century world.

Saul of Tarsus went early in life to Jerusalem to study under Gamaliel, a teacher of the Pharisaic party. This rabbinical training was very obvious in Paul's later approach to the scriptures and in his method of reasoning. Since rabbinical students were also required to know a trade by which to support themselves, this could be where Paul's tentmaking comes in. According to Acts of the Apostles, Saul seemed to command respect among the Pharisaic party and took an active part in trying to suppress the new Christian movement by force.

The Road to Damascus

The key to understanding Paul's thought lies in the famous incident on the road to Damascus. Saul set out on that journey as a Pharisee in good standing. His whole life was centred around the Law of God, his whole concern was with keeping that Law in its finest detail. By studying the traditions of the great teachers and putting them into practice, Saul knew that it was possible to please God; like all the Pharisees, Saul had made salvation into a science. But a cloud was darkening Saul's sky: a new heresy based on the teachings of Jesus of Nazareth. These people were threatening many things which Saul and his fellow Pharisees held dear — hadn't they just recently executed one of them, Stephen by name, because he had dared to teach that the Temple was unnecessary and would be destroyed? And now they were beginning to spread their pernicious errors among the Jews of the Diaspora in Damascus. The rot must be stopped, and Saul was the man for the job.

But then Saul got knocked off his high horse in more ways than one. The importance of the event is indicated by the fact that it is recounted three times in Acts, once by Luke as narrator and twice in the reported speeches of Paul himself. The overall effect was that Saul's religious certainty was shaken to its roots: instead of leading him to do God's will, his theological outlook had compelled him to work in opposition to God's plan. This in itself was a lesson which Paul was never to forget. The revelation of Jesus to Saul on the road to Damascus also had another lesson for the would-be-persecutor; it taught Saul that Jesus is present among his followers, so that by persecuting them, Saul was in fact attacking him.

Paul the Missionary

We might have the impression that Paul's mighty ministry began soon after this experience. Paul certainly started preaching in Damascus, the place where he was supposed to be stopping the Christian movement, not encouraging it; but the famous missionary journeys were to be many years off in the future.

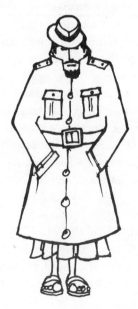

Some people felt Paul made a suspicious type of convert.

Paul doesn't seem to have been very popular as a new Christian. The opponents of Christianity tried to kill him in Damascus, and his fellow Christians found it hard to decide whether he was a genuine convert or an enemy infiltrator. After escaping from Damascus and a mixed reception in Jerusalem, Paul was sent off home to Tarsus, where he seems to have bided his time for quite a few more years. In fact, the only influential Christian who is on record as really believing in Paul's potential was Barnabas; he eventually hunts Paul out and brings him to Antioch where the community is an unusual mixture of Jews and Greeks. After some time in that community, and after a relief mission to the Christians in Judaea, Paul and Barnabas began their first missionary journey.

Each of the missionary journeys was eventful, marked with mighty signs, moderate successes and gigantic failures; but the greatest event of all the journeys happened during the first one, in another Antioch (in Asia Minor, Pisidian Antioch to be precise). Paul and Barnabas had followed the accepted practice of the early missionaries and addressed their message to the Jews during the synagogue service. When they met with strong Jewish resistance in Pisidian Antioch, Paul and Barnabas resolutely turned their efforts towards making converts from the pagans.

The matter of trying to convert the pagans raised such a storm that it took a meeting of church leaders in Jerusalem to settle it.[1] But that was hardly the end of the opposition to what Paul was doing; extremists from among the Jewish Christians seemed to hold that adherence to certain requirements of the Old Testament Law was still binding on Christian converts from paganism. And certain pagan converts were also making unacceptable changes in the gospel which Paul preached. These are the sort of problems which occasioned the letters which have made Paul famous.

Paul's Letters

The letters are arranged in the New Testament according to length, more or less, not according to the order in which they were written. As in the case of other biblical books, the authorship of these documents cannot always be taken at face value. Quite a

---

1. This meeting, and the issues that led to it, are treated in Chapter Seven.

few, such as Romans, First Corinthians and Galatians, would be accepted as Pauline by all scholars; some — like Colossians and Ephesians — would have question marks hanging over them, though opinions would differ. And then a few, notably the two letters to Timothy and the one to Titus, might contain material from letters which had originally come from Paul's hand, but can hardly claim Paul as their author in their present state; this would be in the great biblical tradition of ascribing authorship to the figure whose thought you wish to continue into your own day and circumstances.[2]

Part of the problem in deciding whether a letter belongs to Paul or not is that his theology has a habit of growing. For instance, the correspondence to the Thessalonians is generally accepted as the earliest of the letters, and it demonstrates a concern with the immediacy of Christ's second coming which is absent from the later letters. And Colossians (which many today take to be authentically Pauline) shows a considerable development on such topics as the effect of baptism and the relationship of the church to Christ. Seeing that the letters were written over a span of some fifteen years, we can allow that Paul's theology would undergo some developments.

The Mission to the Gentiles

Some of the more stable elements in Paul's theology stem from his mission to the Gentiles. It is difficult for us to imagine the change in mentality which this required in Paul; we instinctively look upon religion as something which does not recognise national boundaries or racial sub-groups. Yet Judaism was primarily a religion for a people who shared a common ancestry. In the first century, some groups were attempting to convert Gentiles; but even full converts to Judaism did not enjoy all of the rights in their new religion which a full-blooded Israelite did. Now Paul found himself bringing many Gentiles into his new faith — which he saw as the valid continuation of the faith of the Old Testament — and he was accepting them as full members of the faith community

---

2. The Letter to the Hebrews was only attributed to Paul centuries after it was written. Translators and commentators today treat it as an anonymous document which never intended to claim Paul as its author.

without making half as many demands upon them as would have been made if they had converted to Judaism.

The problem was complicated by the opposition which Paul received from some elements in the church. The line of reasoning followed by Paul's opponents went something like this: Jesus the Messiah came in fulfilment of the promises made to the ancestors of Israel; therefore the Messiah is meant for Israel, not for the pagans. If people of pagan stock are to be brought into the church, they must become members of Israel if they are to inherit the promises made to Israel.

Thus far Paul would have few arguments with his opponents' way of thinking. The question which would divide them was how this entry into Israel was to be effected. The opponents would have gone back to Genesis 17 for their answer; they would have pointed out that in this chapter, in which they would also have seen a veiled promise of the Messiah in the statement that royalty would spring from Abraham's seed, every male member of the family and household of Abraham is to be circumcised as a perpetual sign of the covenant with Abraham. Therefore, at a minimum, Paul's opponents were demanding the circumcision of all male converts. On the face of it, they had a strong theological case.

Yet Paul was not willing to demand this of his pagan converts. Circumcision was a matter which kept many interested pagans from becoming full converts in the first place, and to make this demand for Christianity would undoubtedly have had the same effect. Before placing such an outstanding handicap upon his mission, Paul would have to determine whether it was absolutely necessary to do so. And although the problem may not seem much of a burning issue in our day, the answer which Paul found has had a tremendous influence on Christianity ever since; the debates about its implications for us are part of what separates Catholic and Protestant traditions today.

Observance of the Law versus Faith

Paul's answer, which is found in the Letters to the Galatians and to the Romans, was the product of his rabbinical training in the scriptures combined with his vision as a Christian. He, too, goes back to Abraham as the ancestor of Israel and asks whether it really was because of circumcision that Abraham was acceptable to God. And he found that circumcision came after Abraham's acceptability, not before it. What made Abraham the friend of God was to be found in Genesis 15:6: "Abraham put his faith in Yahweh who credited it to him as righteousness". Paul reasoned that circumcision was only a later and less important sign of the new relationship; the deciding factor was Abraham's faith. Once the new converts had faith, then they were part of Abraham's line and household and heirs to all the promises. If they were circumcised and did not have faith, they had no share in Abraham's heritage.

Circumcision and the Law hadn't really accomplished much anyway, Paul observed. Certainly if anyone kept every precept of the Law, they would be most pleasing to God — but who succeeded in doing this anyway? And if we want to depend on our observance of the Law to be right with God, then we have to play the legalistic game fully. Law is not about keeping track of all the times it isn't broken, but about punishing the offences against it. When your car is stopped by sirens and flashing lights for driving at 60 miles per hour in a 30-mile zone, it is no defence to point out to the arresting officer that your driving licence is in order or that you have no drink taken; his only concern will be with the offence. So too, Paul argues, once we have made the slightest infringement of the least of the commandments of the Old Testament Law, we can no longer look to it as our way of standing proud before God. Instead, we must rely on his mercy and forgiveness, which is what faith does.

But if we apply our usual meaning of the term to the faith advocated by Paul we do him a disservice. Faith for us can be confined to the intellect, indicating belief, knowledge which is beyond indisputable proof. The Greek word which Paul uses means this, certainly, yet goes further; it is also the word for trust and faithfulness — not just believing, but being true to that belief with all of one's life. The demands which Paul makes of his converts in their community life and private behaviour shows that it was not simply belief which would turn a pagan into a Christian.

The Law and its demands would have caused serious inconvenience to the new converts and would have deterred countless others from considering the Christian message at all. Observance of the Law was objectionable to Paul on another ground as well: for the Jews living in largely pagan centres of population, the Law acted as a barrier between them and their Gentile neighbours. Jewish customs and dietary regulations meant that social relationships between Jew and Gentile were severely restricted and, in Paul's vision, this was the type of artificial division which Jesus had tried to eliminate. Paul was working to build God's people along new lines which were open to all humanity, not to set up new barriers.

Paul went even further than this, claiming that the strict binding power of the Law was not only ineffectual in achieving its aims and detrimental to the gathering of a new people for the Father, but was broken by the death of Jesus. "Christ set us free from the curse of the Law when he himself became something accursed on our behalf according to its stipulation: 'Anyone hanged on wood is accursed.' (Gal 3:13) A Law which has stated a curse that applies to God's Messiah has relinquished its right to be seen as God's Law; the death of Jesus has rendered the binding force of the Torah invalid so that individuals from many traditions and racial backgrounds can now be grafted into God's people by faith in Jesus.

Naturally, some of Paul's opponents accused him of preaching a gospel of irresponsibility. Even today, some interpret Paul's message as saying that once there is belief in Jesus, the Christian can never lose the salvation offered to believers.

Such people have hardly read Paul with attention! Even in that great charter of Christian liberty, the Letter to the Galatians, Paul warns his hearers that their lifestyle can disqualify them from inheriting the fullness of salvation:

The deeds of the flesh are plainly seen: filth, impurity, debauchery, idolatry, magic, enmity, strife, jealousy, great anger, selfish ambitions, argumentativeness, cliquishness, envy, drunkenness and carousing, and all that sort of thing. I am telling you beforehand, just as I have said it before that those who indulge in such things will not inherit the Kingdom of God. (Gal 5:19-21)

Paul is certainly concerned with morality in his writings, but he would never restrict morality to simply keeping rules and regulations.

Father, Son and Spirit

Once we see that the faith which justifies is not just belief but a trusting faithfulness, then we can see it as a word which speaks of the whole relationship between the Christian and God. Paul perceived this relationship as three-fold, a relationship which we would term Trinitarian today, involving the Father, Son and Spirit.

The New Testament uses the word "God" both as a name and as a title. Some passages, such as Jn 1:1 and 20:28, apply the word as a title to Jesus, indications of the Christian belief in the divinity of Christ. But when "God" appears as a name in the New Testament, it refers to God the Father. This differs somewhat from our common usage, for we can say such things as "When God was on earth ...." or "When God was born at Bethlehem ...." The New Testament reserves that sort of usage for God the Father, and modern readers sometimes have to make an effort to keep that distinction in mind. Paul generally uses the word "Lord" in reference to Jesus, whereas the modern Christian is again capable of confusing things by applying this term to the Father as well as to the Son. The only one who doesn't seem to get confused in matters of terminology between New Testament usage and modern usage is God the Holy Spirit; and perhaps that is because modern Christians rarely speak about him! After that brief effort at clarification, perhaps we are in a better position to see how Trinitarian Paul's outlook is.

> There are different gifts apportioned, but the same Spirit. And there are different services apportioned, and the same Lord. And there are different activities apportioned, but it is the same God who is working everything in everyone. (1 Cor 12:4-6)

It is only a small example, but it demonstrates how Paul sees the workings of the Christian community in the light of this threefold relationship. God the Father is the source and goal of the whole Christian life. He is known and served through Jesus, "the visible image of the unseen God" (Col 1:15), who is the Lord and Master of all believers. And God's actions continue in his people through the activity of the Spirit whom "God has sent into our hearts" (Gal 4:6), making us his children and prompting and enabling us to work for his Kingdom.

Paul's approach is not unlike the modern approach to the Trinity which reflects upon the Christian experience of God as "beyond, beside and within". We recognise that God is different from us, immeasurably greater than anything we are or can become, and that for anything we might know of him, there will always be an infinity which is constantly outside our grasp; this, our experience of the God beyond, is especially apt when speaking of God the Father. Yet, at the same time our experience of God is not one of a deity who is aloof and uncaring; he is, rather, intensely involved with humanity, which is sometimes called his image and likeness (after Gen 1:26). The divine concern with us is not only known by our nature and creation, but also by the message which God addresses to us, culminating in the incarnation of his Son, our experience of God beside us. Through him, we have not only the fullest expression of God's invitation to us, but also the pattern of our response. But again, our experience of the Godhead is more intimate still; there are times when we feel his strength and power, times when his closeness to us is beyond expression. And this experience of the God within is God the Holy Spirit who joins himself to our frailty and transforms it.

This is the structure upon which Paul built his whole approach to what the Christian life should be: centred in the Father, modelled upon the Son, empowered by the Spirit. And he never hesitated to hold it up as the pattern for all Christian thinking, not just his own. To the community of Christians at Philippi, torn and divided by petty power struggles, he quoted from a hymn on the humility of Christ to bring them to their senses (Phil 2:5-11). When the Galatians were attracted by the seemingly religious security of the Law and its demands, Paul responded by reciting the demands of the Christian life as the fruit which the Spirit must be allowed to produce within them (Gal 5:22-23).

The Holy Spirit has a key role in Paul's concept of the Christian life, for his function is to change and guide our lives from within, not from without like the Old Testament Law. "For we all ... are being transformed into the Lord's very image by the Lord Spirit, going from glory to glory." (2 Cor 3:18) If the example of Jesus is outside our reach, the Holy Spirit makes imitation possible, raising us from the level of mere "flesh" to the level of spirit. The gift of the Spirit makes us members of God's family, his children by adoption just as Jesus is the only son by nature. The work of the Spirit continues to dwell with us as we live a life of faithful trust, until his work is complete when we are conformed to the resurrection of Jesus. Much of this activity of the Spirit is woven by Paul into the centrepiece of his Letter to the Romans (Rom 8:1-17).

Paul's Insight into Unity

But the Spirit has another goal to his activity, hinted at in the familar conclusion to Second Corinthians: "The grace of the Lord, Jesus Christ, and the love of God and fellowship of the Holy Spirit be with all of you." (2 Cor 13:13) Another example of Paul's Trinitarian approach! But what is this strange word "fellowship"? Hardly a term which we use every day, and rarely heard outside religious speech. The Greek word is *koinōnia,* meaning a close

Few of us would envy the Holy Spirit his job of achieving Christian unity.

relationship between people, a partnership, a word with overtones of sharing and caring. The Spirit is not just our private intimate experience of God within; he is also our experience of God dwelling in the Christian community. He is the Spirit of unity who tries to draw us together and to build us into a unity of love. All of his gifts and all of his activity have an eye to this end; and when we notice how quick Christians can be to divide and argue and criticise, I think that few of us will envy the Holy Spirit his job.

The ideal of unity gives the theology of Paul much of its thrust. He is not willing to allow the Law to divide Jew and Gentile; he appeals to unity frequently when seeking the answer to difficult practical problems and sees it as the goal of the Holy Spirit working among us. Not surprisingly, unity is also a key concept for Paul when he speaks of the church.

Paul's most famous and most potent image for the church is the Body of Christ; but by body, he did not mean simply the physical side of Christ's humanity, but the whole personality of Christ as it manifests itself through that physical reality. He was saying that the church is the physical presence of Jesus in the world today.

The image was also a convenient one for showing how unity can embrace the manifest differences that exist among Christians in their priorities, personalities and talents. Paul argues that the human body needs its differences, that each limb and organ makes its own unique contribution to the body's life; and the Body of Christ is no different, for it too needs to be enriched through the diversity of its members, each with their different gifts.

The Spirit plays his part in this image; since the human spirit was seen as the life-force of the human body, so the Spirit of Jesus could be seen as the life-force of the Body of Christ. Again, we should be forcibly struck by Paul's connection of the concept of unity to his theology of the Holy Spirit: one Spirit shared by many individuals to draw them together toward a common purpose and the bond of love.

In the later letters of the Pauline collection, the image of the Body of Christ receives a more developed treatment. In the earlier letters of Romans and First Corinthians, the picture is applied primarily to the local church and to its unity. But in Colossians and Ephesians, it is the worldwide church which is under consideration. The person of Jesus received no special treatment in the schema of First Corinthians, but now he is spoken of as the Head of the Body into whose likeness the rest of the Body must mature and grow. This allocation of the role of Head to Christ himself allows the stress to fall on another part of the image: we are only joined to Jesus by being joined to one another.

If we are sincere in our love, we shall grow through everything into Christ who is himself the Head. From him the whole Body has been joined together, brought together by means of every joint, supplying the growth of the Body through the action of each and every member, each according to his own measure, for its own up-building in love. (Eph 4:15-16)

Baptism for Paul is at once an entry into the church and a joining to Christ, especially in his death and resurrection. Membership of the Body of Christ makes its own demands on the way Christians live; they are no longer their own property, but members of Christ's Body, making everything that they do reflect for good or ill on Christ himself (1 Cor 6:15-20). Our union with the sacrificed and risen Lord gives us the direction which our goals should take:

So if you have been raised up with Christ, look for the things above where Christ is, seated at God's right hand. Concentrate on the things above, not on worldly affairs. For you have died, and your life is now hidden with Christ in God's presence. When Christ, your life, is revealed, then too you shall be revealed with him in. glory. So put to death those parts of yourself which are purely worldly. (Col 3:1-5)

The Body also supplied another image for showing how Jew and Gentile can be brought together into unity despite their former divisions. Although it was a great privilege to be born into membership of Israel, membership of Christ is now to be seen as the greatest possible participation in God's plan of salvation. Pagan and Jew, once divided to the point of hatred, are now becoming incorporated into one body, a unity so great that all former differences fade away (Eph 2:11-18).

Paul's last years are unknown to us. Acts of the Apostles only brings the life of Paul as far as his first imprisonment in Rome. Did that imprisonment end in his execution? Luke gives us no indication that it did. Did Paul ever fulfil the plan he mentioned at the end of Romans to preach in Spain? There is no evidence that compels us to believe that he ever touched that shore. What we do know is that one day in the decade of the sixties, he witnessed to the gospel he had preached by giving his life outside Rome on the road to Ostia. But not before this theologian and tentmaker had impressed forever upon Christianity his unyielding idealism and its imperative practicality.

Finishing with a Bang

APOCALYPTIC

EVERY devotee knows what to expect from his or her favourite soap opera. A good soap opera demands a family or two, many members of which have crises and problems, a tangle of involved emotional relationships, and a healthy sprinkling of characters who are pleasing to the eye. And the viewer who settles down comfortably in front of the telly knows instinctively that a fortnight's gossip from the local neighbourhood would never compare with what is about to be seen packed into one episode, served up on the television's electronic platter.

But imagine a person who knows nothing about soap operas and who had never before encountered acting and drama. What would this uninitiated viewer make of his or her first encounter with such a programme? Even after it dawned on this unsuspecting mind that the sounds and visions were not broadcasts from real life, other questions would arise: If these scenes are not from real life, can they be said to be typical of real experience? If they cannot be said to be typical of real experience, what deeper meaning do soap operas have or what needs do they satisfy? And (most importantly) is there anything better on the other channels?

A Strange kind of Writing

We are at somewhat the same type of disadvantage when we approach the apocalyptic literature of the Bible; the very word "apocalyptic" is strange to us, and the form of writing it represents is even stranger. "Apocalyptic" comes from a Greek word which means unveiling; the purpose of apocalyptic literature is to show the real workings of God's plan in the present by

Apocalyptic will always be popular with a certain type of people.

revealing the future to which history is moving. It is an art form now lost to us. People still feel sufficiently comfortable with some of the biblical forms to continue imitating them; for instance, modern psalms and modern parables abound, even though their form has evolved from that of their scriptural counterparts. But who is still composing apocalyptic literature today? In fact, the heyday of this type of writing was limited to the two centuries or so immediately before and after Christ. Since that time the apocalyptic literature in the Bible (largely parts of Zechariah and Daniel in the Old Testament and Revelation, sometimes called the Apocalypse, in the New) has proved to be the most unpopular writing in the scriptures along with Leviticus, Numbers and a few genealogical listings.

Unpopular, that is, except with a certain type of people. Apocalyptic literature, and especially the Book of Revelation, provides a happy hunting ground for every class of religious fanatic and ample quotations for the tracts of bizarre cults. Since we have lost touch with apocalyptic's mode of expression, our difficulties in appreciating its message have largely discouraged us from reading it. Yet where problems of understanding increase, so too do the possibilities of misinterpretation. So the language of apocalyptic has been twisted and hammered until it is claimed that it proves just about anything from God as a spaceman to the doctrine that Christ's second coming actually occurred at the beginning of this century.

If the beginning reader turns to apocalyptic at all, it is often in fulfilment of that ancient human curiosity about the end of the world, combined with a certain predilection for bad news. Whatever good it will do them, people do seem to want to know when the end will occur. The people of Rome have provided themselves with two signs in their folk-belief: when the circuit of the Colosseum's oval is broken and when all of the gilt is worn away from the statue of Marcus Aurelius on the Capitoline, then the end will come. Other inhabitants of the globe, for whom the cost of travelling to Rome in order to investigate these helpful omens is prohibitive, indulge their fatalistic curiosity by opening these dark and mysterious pages of apocalyptic.

Yet to read apocalyptic with the impression that its main purpose is to tell the reader about the end of the world is to do it a grave injustice. The end of the world is a gloomy subject, and many of the images surrounding it in apocalyptic literature are tragic; but the central theme and underlying message of apocalyptic is centred on hope. Unless we look for the hope in a piece of apocalyptic writing we will miss the author's point and misread his work.

A Literature of Hope

As in many matters biblical, we must place ourselves back in the time of these writings in order to appreciate them. The few centuries in which apocalyptic flourished were times of hopelessness; it had become clear to most religious people that God was allowing his people to suffer political humiliation and religious persecution nearly beyond endurance. Whereas according to more ancient Old Testament thinking, God would reward the virtuous in this life, many of the pious were the victims of severe oppression, some even to the point of martyrdom. People caught in these dire straits were tempted to ask whether God's plan for his people had failed; would the forces of evil triumph, as they seemed poised to do? The answer was framed in terms of the apocalyptic literature.

Apocalyptic conceived of two realities in its world-view: the present, which was dominated by the forces of evil, and the future, which would be totally under God's control. And even though the present is dominated by evil, in the view of apocalyptic everything is really working according to a divine plan. Evil is under the illusion that it will possess the victory, and appearances seem to verify that illusion; yet only God knows where things are heading and sees how present events are hastening the advent of his glorious reign.

Now, since the present gives a false impression on the surface and since God alone knows how his plan is really at work in what is happening, he reveals his future to chosen individuals in visions which show the true nature of current affairs. The chosen messenger then, in turn, reveals God's plan to those who will hear it with understanding.

But essentially God's plan remains a secret, something hidden from the eyes of the godless and the ears of the apathetic. The message is never a simply prosaic interpretation of world events but is often encoded — as secrets should be — in symbols and imagery which will protect it from those without understanding. The effort required to pierce its veil will aid the reader in piercing the thicker veil covering the reality around him which he must face and interpret properly.

Apocalyptic literature spoke, first and foremost, to people of wavering hope, those tempted to abandon their ancestral faith, which could no longer offer them dreams of worldly success and achievement, in favour of the Hellenistic paganism which could. The classical prophets could speak their message more plainly, and when they referred to the future it was usually in terms of realistic developments from the present. But the milieu of apocalyptic was tinted with no such gleams of light; if God's action was to be seen, it had to manifest itself in new and overt ways. And this concept of the action of God which would be so outstanding that it would break with the known patterns of history and render them useless was also part of the apocalyptic vision. This end to history's story, like the happy ending of a novel, would give meaning to the whole saga, even to what appears to be, in the present, meaningless suffering, defeat and hopelessness.

Many works of apocalyptic literature written during this time never made it into the canon of Scripture. There is no doubt that much of this literature played its part by sustaining the hope of God's people in times of extreme suffering and trials. Some of it is useful today for the light it throws onto the period of the New Testament. But our attention will be focused on the strains of apocalyptic which can be found in the pages of the New Testament.

Christian Apocalyptic

Early Christian experience led to the conclusion that the will and plan of God was not being fully implemented in the present moment. Whereas earlier apocalyptic writing could speak as if the appearance of the Messiah would in itself bring in the era of bliss for God's people, Christians were saying that something else had taken place: even though Jesus, God's Messiah, had come, he was not a figure of power bringing vast material wealth to Israel. He was a figure of suffering and rejection, plotted against and killed. Even after the resurrection, those who accepted him as Messiah formed only a small minority; and they often continued to experience the same type of rejection — and even persecution —with which Jesus himself had been received.

Yet a cornerstone of their proclamation was that things would change. The time would come when God's will would be put into full effect, when Jesus would be seen as the Messiah of power and blessing, when his followers would enjoy the bountiful harvest of all the Old Testament promises. This time was centred on the second coming of Jesus, one of the bare essentials in the message of the first missionaries.

It is easy to see from that how the apocalyptic view of two realities (a present which is not completely under God's control and a future which would be) was found meaningful in the early church. But apocalyptic writing went further; the future would only arrive after a struggle between the forces of evil which now seem to predominate and the power of God. This struggle would have cataclysmic effects in the human world, causing horrendous suffering to bad and good alike, yet in the end ensuring that evil is rendered powerless and allowing the complete plan of God to reign without further interference. This picture emphasises to the reader that the power of evil poses a formidable threat which must, of necessity, be overcome in a formidable manner.

Sometimes the modern reader is overly startled by this aspect of apocalyptic thinking, hypnotised by the imagery. If we delay too long at this aspect of apocalyptic, we might get the impression that it is a very gloomy and fearful type of writing; yet, as has been stressed before, apocalyptic writing is the literature of hope. The terrors are only a preamble to the real heart of its message, which is the time of God's reign, the eternal calm after the storm. Our misreading of apocalyptic thinking in the New Testament betrays itself whenever we speak of the second coming of Christ as the end of the world; apocalyptic would see it as more of a beginning.

Many of these elements can be seen in 2 Thess 1:7-2:12 or Mk 13:3-37. Both of these passages link the sufferings and rejection which Christians experience in the present with what must happen before the conflict between God and evil comes to a head. They both refer to the power of evil as a person who will show himself more clearly when the struggle reaches its climax, and both assure that the victory is in God's hands, as will be seen when Jesus appears in power. There is also a note to the effect that keeping faith during the final scenes of the conflict will require a special clarity of vision and a shrewd interpretation of events.

The Book of Revelation

Even though apocalyptic thought and writing is to be found in many sections of the New Testament, there is only one complete work of apocalyptic literature in the list of New Testament books. And very few would weep if it should miraculously disappear from that list in the morning. The Book of Revelation is undoubtedly the most problematic book in the Christian scriptures, and no modern interpreter can claim to have solved its many riddles. Yet enough is known about it to allow it to be read with profit and to let the main themes of its message be heard today. Space will not allow us even

John the Seer wrote his book in code.

to skim the surface of its deep waters; we must content ourselves with little more than an aerial photograph.

The author of Revelation gives his name as John, which has led many to associate this book with the Gospel of John; yet the style and thought of the two works are so different that it is apparent that the two books come from different people. Instead of imagining the author of Revelation to be the disciple John, we should think of him as another John from the early church; here he shall be referred to simply as "John the Seer", a Jewish Christian visionary of the late first century.

John tells us much about the condition of his communities in the seven letters which open his work. We see, for instance, that it was a time of trial, and there are indications that Christians are under pressure to partake of the emperor cult; one martyr to the cause is named (Rev 2:13) which may indicate that a local persecution was in progress. Unfortunately the seven letters also make it clear that these communities did not always respond with unwavering faithfulness; they compromised with the emperor cult, mingled their faith with pagan practices, and indulged in crass materialism. John the Seer presents his book to them as an aid to

125

purifying their outlook and to regaining their commitment.

The modern reader need hardly be told that John the Seer wrote his book in code! Sometimes we can see through the code easily enough; for example, in chapter five an unnamed lamb appears as the one worthy to break the seals, and no Christian has difficulty in identifying that Lamb as Jesus. But the code is not always so easy. Some of his code is drawn from the common imagery of his day, so that his ancient reader would have readily seen the harlot seated on seven hills as Rome (which was built on seven hills), or the eagle in Rev 8:13 as the Roman representation of its chief deity, Jupiter. But some of this common imagery is undoubtedly lost on the modern commentator, which is one of the factors which makes Revelation such an elusive book.

Numbers are also used symbolically by John the Seer. Seven is the number of divine perfection, just as six is the number of dangerous imperfection and of the satanic imitation of the divine. Four stands for the whole world, and twelve is the number of God's people. Even multiples and factors can be used in a symbolic way: the hundred and forty-four thousand in chapter seven are not the quota of the saved, but the perfection of God's people (twelve times twelve times a thousand). So combining the text of the Apocalypse and your pocket calculator is a futile exercise if you are trying to discover the date of the earth's demise!

John the Seer draws heavily from the realm of worship for his images. Not only does the heavenly worship accompany all of the mighty scenes in Revelation, but symbols such as trumpets, bowls, and the lamb itself come from the liturgies of the Jerusalem Temple. The Christian liturgy is also used by John; more than one interpreter has noticed that his vision of heaven in chapter four is modelled on the arrangement of the local church when it gathered to celebrate the Sunday Eucharist. One message which John communicated by his use of the language of liturgy is that our communal worship links us to the mighty acts of God, to his plan taking shape in our own time.

But none of the code of Revelation could be understood without the Old Testament. John's quotations of it are not excessive, but he continually draws images from it, sometimes changing them slightly for his new picture. He uses Daniel's beast and Ezekiel's Temple, presuming that his reader will have been acquainted with their meaning in the Old Testament and thus be able to transfer that old meaning to new situations.

The complex code of Revelation makes it necessary to read the work today with either a commentary or a comprehensive set of notes. Yet when this is done, two interesting things emerge: the first is how the Seer unmasks contemporary affairs for his readers, showing that the Roman Empire is not a friend but a beast, enemy of God and of his church, and how God's beleaguered people are really the victors; the second is how skilfully John brings Old Testament images and themes to new heights in light of Christ. It may be an accident of history that Revelation is the last book in the Bible, but is is a fitting place for it since it gives a final dimension to so many of the pictures of the scriptures.

We are unfair to the Apocalypse when we think of it as being about the end of the world. Its climax is not the end, but the beginning of God's new creation, the founding of God's eternal city where humanity shall set up its home with the Lord. John the Seer knows that there are rough times ahead for the church, but his gaze is fixed on the good things to follow. So, even after his graphic descriptions of what God's people must go through, he can still conclude his book with a cry, "Come, Lord Jesus"; it is worth it, John is saying. Let God's kingdom come, even if it does mean the end of many things to which we have become attached.

The Lessons of Apocalyptic

It is to be regretted that modern Christians ignore the apocalyptic literature of the Bible because of its difficulties and its openness to misuse and misinterpretation. Apocalyptic has much to teach us; without it, our biblical vision loses a colour in its spectrum. Perhaps the remaining paragraphs of this chapter might be spent in trying to describe this often unseen hue.

First, despite appearances, the message of apocalyptic literature and thought has to do with the present rather than with the future. But just as no story can be interpreted without knowing its ending, so apocalyptic writing tries to show the meaning of the present by revealing the end of history's story. When this is done, it becomes clearer that the surface meaning of world affairs can be misleading:

those now in control, seeming to frustrate the divine plan as it suits them, are destined to be overthrown; forces which might superficially seem to be innocuous or even benign can, upon close inspection, become visible as manifestations of the darkest powers of evil. Apocalyptic literature challenges the Christian to examine the world constantly with the critical eye of faith.

Apocalyptic's concern with the present — even though its language is often future — is part of its conviction that God's plan is at work, even in the worst events and most disastrous setbacks which the people of God might experience. Apocalyptic knows that what happens in the here and now really matters, that somehow every part of the Christian life (be it suffering or worship or triumph) helps to move history along towards the new creation. We are also warned not to confuse the present with God's plan fully at work — we are told again and again that not everything is rosy in the human garden — but we are also assured that we will benefit from its full effect when it comes.

If apocalyptic encourages hope and supports fainthearted faith, it also launches a full-blown attack on complacency. The worst choice that the Christian can make is to place his hopes in the present rather than in God's future. That is the seedbed of compromise and the lukewarm response, the sure prospect that the gospel vision will be distorted through a lens of comfort and security. To the apocalyptic mind there is only one way to be realistic, and that is to have the sights set firmly on God's promise and plan, for it is certainly going to be fulfilled.

Perhaps the religious fanatics who use Daniel and Revelation to tell us that the world will end next Monday have so damaged the reputation of apocalyptic literature that it will never recover. It would be a pity, for this strange and exotic writing has so much to offer us still. Apocalyptic brings to a climax the prophets' critical view of their society, wisdom literature's dissatisfaction with the lot of the just and devout, the gospels warning that this world and its values have no claim to permanence. Without the vision of apocalyptic, Christians become too comfortable with the way things are. We begin to place our hope in human structures and events, aligning ourselves too readily to this political system or that economic philosophy. We are even prepared to slaughter the children of God in warfare on the blasphemous assumption that God is on our side.

As modern Christians, we still need the message of apocalyptic that the world around us is not enough. We need a healthy suspicion that the answers it so glibly offers and the philosophy it expounds fall short of the vision of the gospel. The medicine of apocalyptic writing might seem bitter at times, but it is necessary if our deepest longings as Christians are to be reawakened; only then will we look to God for the fulfilment of our hope.

Opening the Scriptures

HINTS FOR READING

AT this point, we have come to the end of our brief tour of the Bible's landscape. We have looked at many of the major attractions and even made one or two excursions into territory which is often untouched by the first-time visitor.

Hopefully, you will feel like paying a few return visits to some of the sights we have glimpsed. How you do that is really up to yourself. Some people will be content to apply the insights which they have received from this book to the readings they hear at the Sunday liturgy; if these few chapters have helped some of the lectionary readings speak more clearly, then they have served their purpose well. The more energetic might want to engage in a more detailed study of Scripture either through using some of the works mentioned at the end of this book or through joining a Bible study group. They will find that their efforts, no matter how small or how great, are well rewarded.

But this chapter is especially for those who would like to start reading Scripture at home, deepening their knowledge and appreciation of the Bible by reading its text. This book has not been written in such a way that the reader is required to turn to the scriptural page every few paragraphs, so perhaps the best thing to do now is to take the plunge into the Bible itself.

But first, you will need a Bible. If you were to ask which of the many translations on the market is the best, I would say to you what experts are expected to say whenever such an honest and straightforward question is posed: "There is no single answer to a question like that." That is partly because of the wide variety of bibles available, the differing types and tastes of the people who

will read them, and the different uses to which they will be put. The purpose of these few pages is to help you decide which version of Scripture is most suited to you and to your needs, not to make that choice for you.

Evaluating Translations

We can begin by making a short-list of those translations which are most in use today and most likely to be considered. They are:

Revised Standard Version (RSV)
Jerusalem Bible (JB)
New International Version (NIV)
New American Bible (NAB)
New English Bible (NEB)
Good News Bible (also called *Today's English Version*/TEV)

A few others have been omitted from this list intentionally, such as the *Authorised Version* (or *King James Version*) and the *Douai-Reims Version*. These translations, nearly four centuries old, might have sentimental attachments for some readers, but can hardly be recommended today; most of Scripture — especially the books of the New Testament — was written in the everyday language of the people to whom it was first addressed. To read it now in an English which is archaic does the Bible a disservice and muffles its message. The so-called *Living Bible* is also left out of this list since it is not a translation or version at all; it is one man's paraphrase of the *Authorised Version* and contains more than one idea which would have surprised the biblical writers! It has no place in our considerations.

Whatever other considerations we might have, when investigating these translations we will be looking for the twin virtues of readability and accuracy; be forewarned — there is no translation which combines the two in perfect balance. It is hardly possible that such a translation could exist, since the rhythms, modes of expression and vocabulary of one language never have exact equivalents in another. Unless the English version is going to be nearly unintelligible, some of the nuances and ambiguities of the original must be sacrificed; unless the richness of the original is going to be decimated, no translation will read as smoothly and clearly as a document originally written in the language we speak.

On readability, the highest score must go to the *Good News Bible;* and, as might be expected, it gets one of the lower scores on accuracy. If a reader were using it to make theological points by quoting a verse or two, the question of accuracy might demand a different version; yet, on the whole, it is reliable enough. If you are trying to read a long section of Scripture at one sitting, or if you are looking for a bible that uses a language that young people can understand, then the *Good News Bible* would be the natural choice. It is attractively produced and has a number of aids for the beginning reader — not least of which are the pleasant line drawings to be found in most editions. The Catholic reader should ensure that it is the edition with the Apocrypha (or Deuterocanonical Books) which is purchased; otherwise some of the books of the Old Testament (such as Wisdom and Sirach) will be missing.

Accuracy is a more elusive quality in a translation. To many people, it means a word-for-word correspondence between the original language text and its English rendition; yet such a notion of accuracy can often lose the natural rhythms and impact which brought the original to life, and a freer translation can be truer in fact. But word-for-word correspondence has its uses, especially for a close study of a passage, and for that reason such translations often serve as the basis for commentaries which treat a work verse by verse. The *Revised Standard Version* is the most popular of such translations, and its dependence on the *Authorised Version* makes it a great favourite with those who like a traditional ring to their Scripture.

Unfortunately, the present edition of this scholarly translation retains archaic language in passages which are addressed to God, introducing an artificiality which was unknown in the original texts. Again, as might be expected, the *Revised Standard Version* would not get honourable mention for readability; if this is the major concern, a different version is called for. There are two editions of this translation which are especially suitable for Catholic readers, the *Revised Standard Version Catholic Edition* and the *Common Bible,* an ecumenical edition arranged for use by all Christians whether Catholic or Protestant or Orthodox. Editions of the RSV with aids for the reader are rare enough, but a fine exception to the rule is the *Oxford Annotated Bible,* available with the Apocrypha. Reader's Digest have also produced a condensed version of the RSV Bible, entitled the *Reader's Bible,* but it falls into the same category of a "non- translation, non-Bible", as does the *Living Bible,* and should not be touched.

The *New International Version* also opts for a word-for-word correspondence with the original, but without the archaisms of the RSV. On the whole, it would score slightly higher on readability, yet its philosophy of translation varies from book to book in the Old Testament. There are no editions with study aids or explanatory notes, nor any editions suitable for use by Catholics (that is, with the deuterocanonical books, or Apocrypha). It could be found useful for the beginner as a second translation for comparison with the translation that the reader normally uses, especially if this is one of the freer versions (such as the *Good News Bible*).

The three remaining translations all aim more for the middle ground between accuracy and readability, with varying degrees of success. The *New English Bible* set out to produce the Bible in timeless English and ended up with an unhappy mixture of the contemporary and the archaic. It has other faults as well; the doctrinal stances of its translators sometimes mar the accuracy of the finished product, and in some parts of the Old Testament the translators seem to have almost composed their own original Hebrew text in defiance of all the norms of scholarship. It is usually published in editions without aids or explanatory notes, but the deuterocanonical books may be found in editions "with the Apocrypha".

For purposes of public reading to adult audiences, one could hardly do better than the *Jerusalem Bible.* And for good reason: the novelist J.R.R. Tolkien was among those who advised on its English style. Its accuracy lapses here and there, but overall it remains a faithful rendition of the original in a highly readable English translation. It is a work produced for Catholic readers of the Bible — and so there is no problem about editions which lack the deuterocanonical books. The *Standard Edition* of the *Jerusalem Bible* has extensive notes and cross-references which make it an ideal study bible, but there are also less expensive editions with short introductions and a minimum of explanatory notes. The *Jerusalem Bible* translation is the one incorporated into the Lectionary for Ireland and Great Britain (although isolated parishes may still be using an older lectionary based on the RSV), and that is a consideration for those who wish to become better acquainted with Scripture in the translation which they hear from Sunday to Sunday.

The *New American Bible* is another Catholic production which attempts to walk the tightrope between accuracy and readability. The list of its translators includes some of the most respected names in American Catholic biblical scholarship of the sixties and early seventies. Although the English style of the NAB is not as literary as the *Jerusalem Bible,* it is quite readable and generally reliable. There are informative introductions to the biblical books, some cross-references to other relevant passages and brief explanatory notes which the beginning reader will find helpful. To this writer's knowledge, it is the only Catholic bible which is available in a giant print edition for those with slightly impaired vision.

Other Considerations

The translation is the major factor in choosing a bible, but it is not the only one. A mistake often made in the past was to choose a bible so large and lavish that there was little chance that it would ever be used for reading purposes. Try to pick one with a print size that is legible and will not cause your knees to tire under the strain of supporting it. Don't indulge in false economy when it comes to choosing the binding; a paperback bible might have an attractive price tag, but it will not hold up to much use. If you hope to use your bible frequently (and let's hope that you do!), then you might give consideration to one of the more expensive bindings — imitation leather or even real leather. These bindings will stand up to years more wear and tear than a cloth binding and so may represent a financial saving in years to come.

Presuming that you have chosen your bible and have spent a few minutes exploring its general layout, you are now in a position to become an authentic Bible reader. But before you do this, may I be permitted to offer a few words of advice?

1. The Bible is a big volume. Don't be greedy. Be content to nibble, taking a little at a time, enjoying it, savouring it. Never worry about the huge amount that has yet to be read; it will still be there when you are ready for it.

2. Concentrate on reading the Bible itself rather than books about the Bible. These are helpful only when Scripture is being read; they are no substitute for the Word of God, but simply help in letting the message of that Word come through.

3. Have a plan for your reading instead of pecking here and there. Try working through a biblical book or at least a healthy section of one to get its feel. If you find that the particular book that you have started is very heavy going, move on to a different one; you can come back to the first one later when you are ready for it. The passages listed in the following section of this chapter also represent a plan of attack.

4. Don't keep to those few parts that you know and like. There is no surer way to get a warped notion of the message of Scripture. Stray into unfamiliar territory from time to time, for knowledge of any part of the Bible enriches your reading of any other part.

5. Ponder what you read. Let it break into your thoughts at different times of the day. Don't be afraid to talk about what you have found meaningful with those who are close to you. *But never use the Bible to win an argument or to condemn someone else's actions; that's not what Scripture is there for.* As an ancient hermit once noted, the message of Scripture is to be applied chiefly to one's own life, not to someone else's life. ("Oh, if Mrs Humperdink could only read this passage, it would show her a thing or two...")

6. Mark your bible every time you read it. Underline the words and phrases that strike you as particularly meaningful. As you become more used to your bible, you might also want to write a word or two in the margin to bring out the theme of a

passage, or a reference to another passage in the Scriptures which is pertinent to the one that you are reading. Several markers are available for highlighting a printed text (although make sure that the ink won't penetrate the paper of your bible), but just about any writing implement will serve the purpose at a pinch. When you return to that passage (or even find yourself trying to locate it again) you won't be sorry that you were brave enough to mark it the first time around.

The passages that follow are loosely based on the chapters of this book and are arranged in sections which correspond to those chapters. They are suggestions for sampling the biblical material in much the same way that it has been treated earlier; use them as you will. If you want to cover all of them, you will have at the end a fair idea of the range of material that lies between the Bible's covers. Take them in any order you choose, perhaps marking those which you have read if you take them in a different order from the one in which they are presented.[1] A brief descriptive note is attached to each passage, and additional information is often available in the relevant chapter of this book if you wish to refer back to it. Try to begin and end each period of reading with a prayer, no matter how short; the Holy Spirit is our main aid in reading and understanding God's Word.

Old Testament History and Torah

These passages will give the reader some idea of the Old Testament's own view of the history of Israel; they were not written primarily to record facts, but to chronicle God's plan working itself out in the arena of human events. Since so much of the Torah is woven into this telling of Israel's story, the references to material from the Pentateuch have also been listed here.

---

1. It might be noted that these readings do not always follow the chapter divisions that we are used to. The division into chapters only came into force in the Middle Ages (and into verses in Reformation times) and do not always follow the sense of the original. Permission is given to make copies of these lists of passages for personal use.

Don't be greedy.

Read the Bible itself, not books about the Bible.

Have a plan for your reading.

Don't keep to those parts you know and like.

Ponder what you read.

Mark your bible every time you read it.

Gen 12:1-9	The call of Abraham.
Gen 15	The covenant with Abraham.
Gen 22	The sacrifice of Abraham.
Ex 3	Yahweh reveals himself to Moses.
Ex 11-12	Passover night in Egypt.
Ex 14-15	Liberation at the Red Sea.
Ex 19,20,24	The great covenant at Sinai.
Josh 24	A covenant after the conquest of Canaan.
Judg 2	The dark ages of Israel before the kings.
Ruth	A story of tenderness set in those hard times.
1 Sam 16-17	The rise of David.
2 Sam 7	The promise to King David.
1 Kings 3	The wisdom of Solomon.
1 Kings 11-12	The follies of Solomon and the start of the divided kingdom.
2 Kings 17	The fall of the northern kingdom.
2 Kings 21-23	Good and bad among Judah's last kings.
2 Kings 24-25	The fall of the southern kingdom.
Ezra 1	Return from exile.
1 Macc 1-2	The start of the Maccabean revolt.

Other material from the Torah:

Gen 1-3	The two stories of creation.
Ex 21-23	Detailed laws from the covenant.
Lev 19	Rules of holiness (and ritual cleanliness) from the Priestly tradition.
Deut 6	Interior attitudes towards God and his law.
Deut 28-30	These curses and blessings show how Israel saw its history in terms of its response to God.

The Worship of Israel

---

1 Kings 8	The consecration of Solomon's Temple.
Lev 23	The great feasts.
Ps 22,80,88,130	A variety of prayers from people in distress.
Ps 40,107,124	Prayers of thanksgiving.
Ps 23,91,121,131	Prayers of trust and confidence.
Ps 113,148,150	Hymns of praise from the Temple.
Ps 2,45,72,110,118	Psalms for royal occasions.
Ps 105	A psalm centred on Israel's history.
Ps 119	A psalm about the gift of the Torah.
Ps 73	A wisdom psalm which contemplates the problem of the wealthy who are godless.

The Prophets

---

1 Kings 22:1-28	True and false prophets at work in the royal court.
Amos 2:6-16	God's accusation against the northern kingdom.
Amos 5:18-6:14	Three woes for Israel, directed to the unjust, the falsely religious and the complacent.
Amos 7:10-17	The prophet shows that his message is not his, but Yahweh's, by relating his call from his former way of life.
Amos 9:8-15	The message of hope which concludes the book of Amos.
Hos 1-3	The disastrous marriage of the prophet and its implications for unfaithful Israel.
Hos 11:1-4,8-9	The tenderness of Yahweh's love.
Is 1:1-2:5	Judah's sinfulness and the vision of future peace.
Is 7	An arrogant king provokes an oracle of a humble king to come.

Is 9:1-6	The restoration of Israel's fortunes under the future king.
Is 11:1-9	Another picture of the reign of the ideal king, perhaps composed by a later disciple of Isaiah.
Is 40	The message of comfort from Second Isaiah at the end of the exile.
Is 44:9-20	Second Isaiah's satire on idol worship.
Is 52:13–53:12	The greatest of the songs of Yahweh's Servant to be found in Second Isaiah.

Wisdom Literature

Practical Advice and Everyday Affairs:

Prov 22:17-24:22	A collection of wise sayings which has much in common with the wisdom traditions in Egypt.
Sir 6:5-17	Observations on true and false friends.
Sir 14:3-19	Warnings against miserliness.
Sir 19:5-16	Discretion and speech.
Sir 31:12-31	Matters of food and drink.
Sir 41:1-13	Contemplating death.

Problematic Wisdom:

Qoh 1-2	The emptiness of life.
Qoh 8:10 — 9:10	The problem of the theory of retribution and Qoheleth's message (Qoh 9:7-10).
Job 1-3	The beginning of Job's story and his first complaint.
Job 15-21	An example of the debate between Job and his friends.
Job 38-39	Yahweh tells Job that he knows what he is doing.
Job 42	The ending to Job's story.
Wis 1-5	Another view on suffering and oppression in the light of life after death.

The Nature of Wisdom

Job 28	Human accomplishments are great, but wisdom remains outside humanity's grasp.
Prov 8	Lady Wisdom sings her praises and invites all who hear to share her treasures.
Sir 24	Lady Wisdom has come to dwell with God's people and is known through the Torah.

New Testament History

Acts 2	The church begins its work in Jerusalem.
Acts 6	The Hellenists and the antagonism with which they are met.
Acts 8:1–25	The gospel spreads to Samaria.
Acts 8:26–40	Three pictures of the good news being brought to the pagans.
Acts 15	The meeting of the church in Jerusalem to decide the question of pagan converts.
Acts 28:14–31	The gospel finally arrives in the capital of the world.

The Gospels

The best advice that anyone can give the beginner about reading a gospel is to choose one of the four and to read it at one sitting. Try not to let the familiarity of many of the stories influence the way you read and if questions about particular passages arise, let them rest until you have finished the entire reading. The important thing is to let the picture of Jesus which the particular evangelist wishes to present emerge clearly in your mind, even if you do have questions about details of his picture. Mark's Gospel has the simplest structure, and lends itself to this experiment; but do not be afraid to attempt it with one of the other gospels.

The following passages are not intended as a substitute for the complete reading of a gospel, but as a supplement. They give a sampling of the style and concerns of each of the four gospels in turn.

Mk 8:27–10:52	Jesus makes the journey to the cross in Jerusalem and teaches his disciples along the way.
Mt 5-7	The Sermon on the Mount, the great compendium of Jesus' teaching as found in Matthew.
Mt 10	The discourse to the twelve apostles as they begin their work of spreading the Kingdom of Heaven.
Mt 13	Parables about the Kingdom of Heaven with its mixture of good and bad, success and failure.
Mt 18	The life of discipleship with a special emphasis on community.
Mt 23-25	The final discourse, including the failure of religious leaders in Jesus' time, the end of Jerusalem, the coming of the Son of Man, and parables about what we should be doing in the meantime.
Lk 10:25-37	A story which breaks down barriers.
Lk 11:5-13	Persisting in prayer.
Lk 15	Three parables on forgiveness for the sinner.
Lk 16:19-31	Warnings about wealth and about not listening to the scriptures.
Lk 18:9-14	A parable on being right with God.
Jn 1:1-18	John's gospel story in a handful of verses.
Jn 6	A sign and its meaning.
Jn 13-17	Jesus' Last Supper and final message for the disciples.

Paul

Acts 9:1-30	Paul's conversion and cool reception.
Philippians	A short letter which makes a fine introduction to Paul's ministry and vision of the Christian life. In its present state it may be a combination of a few shorter letters or parts of letters.

Gal 2:15–4:7   The keeping of the Law is contrasted with justification by faith.

Rom 3:21–5:11   Those who are justified with God are people of faith who depend on what God does for them, not on what they think that they do for God.

Gal 5:13–26   The life of the Spirit contrasted with an earthbound life.

Rom 12   A sample of Paul's teaching on Christian living.

Rom 8   Our relationship with God: Father, Son and Spirit.

1 Cor 12:1–27   The church as Body of Christ.

Col 1   Jew and Gentile brought together into the Body of Christ who is Lord of the Cosmos.

Eph 1:7–2:10; 4:1–16 A later development of the theme of the Body of Christ by a writer who continues Paul's thinking.

Apocalyptic Literature

Since the beginning reader will be unfamiliar with this type of writing, only a few passages are suggested here. More fruitful exploration nearly demands a close reading of these writings with the aid of a reliable commentary, such as Adela Yarbro Collins' *The Apocalypse* in the New Testament Message series (Veritas, 1979).

Dan 7   A vision of four terrifying kingdoms which would give way to the reign of God's people. The imagery of this passage is also used by the book of Revelation.

2 Thess 1:7–2:12 Present troubles are seen in the light of a building up of evil which takes place before the second coming of Christ.

Mk 13:3–37   This passage forewarns of troubles and persecutions both in the context of the destruction of Jerusalem and of the second coming of Jesus at the end of time. The opening vision of the Apocalypse (the risen Christ as high priest) and the letters to the seven churches set the tone for the whole book. These chapters give us many insights into the situation for which the book of Revelation was written and state the warnings and promises which the author hopes that we will take to heart.

Rev 1-3

These chapters give the modern reader the clearest picture of what apocalyptic writing is all about: the glorious future which God has in store for his people, despite the troubles which they must endure in the present.

Rev 21-22

For Further Reading

Towards the end of the Book of Qoheleth there is the wise observation, "The production of many books has no end" (Qoh 12:12). And one of the earliest great biblical scholars of the Christian church, St Jerome, said "It is difficult to read everyone who has written about the gospels to start with; and so it is even more difficult to use proper judgement in selecting what is best." A lot of paper has passed under the presses since Jerome's time! The short list of books which is given here has been selected for the beginner who is ready to get down to work with the biblical text itself.

Celine Mangan's *I Am With You* (Michael Glazier, 1975) guides the beginning reader through a small gallery of biblical pictures of God in short, elegantly written chapters, each of which ends with a suggestion for reading in the biblical text. Those readers who are prepared to work a bit harder might be interested in the beautifully produced *How to Read the Old Testament* and *How to Read the New Testament* by Etienne Charpentier (Crossroad, 1982). These books are filled with valuable insights from the realm of modern scholarship, but are written with the beginner in mind, not the expert.

These three works are aimed principally at the individual reader; but it should be remembered that group study of the Bible will bring insights which an individual could never hope to achieve on his or her own. A one-year plan of exploration, with a special emphasis on the Gospel of John, has been set out in William Riley's *The Bible Group: An Owner's Manual* (Ave Maria, 1984). Though intended for groups, an individual reader might also like to follow the study plan which it sets out. I will admit to a certain prejudice in recommending it.

The *Jerusalem Bible (Standard Edition)* has already been mentioned in the treatment of various translations, but it merits a second mention here for its helpful footnotes, introductions and cross-references. The owner of this full edition (published by Doubleday and Co., 1985) is well equipped for a fruitful study of the Bible.

Some readers might wish to launch themselves on a more detailed study of a particular book, and there are several commentary series available for their use; but series which are suitable to the beginner and written by scholars are not always easy to find. Scholars have a nasty habit of writing principally for their fellow scholars. Three series which, by and large, avoid this pitfall are *Old Testament Message* (Carroll Stuhlmueller and Martin McNamara, series editors, published by Michael Glazier and Gill & Macmillan, covering the full Old Testament in twenty-three volumes), *New Testament Message* (Wilfred Harrington and Donald Senior, series editors, published by Michael Glazier and Veritas, covering the New Testament in twenty-two volumes) and *The Collegeville Bible Commentary* (Robert Karris, series editor, published by Liturgical Press and covering the New Testament in eleven large booklets).

The beginner might appreciate a word of warning about a category of books on the Bible whose titles could be misleading. Any beginner might naturally be attracted to a book with a cover which reads "The Old Testament: An Introduction" or "An Introduction to the New Testament." But in these cases, the word "introduction", is being used in a very specialised sense. It does not refer to the type of work written for the uninitiated, as one might think. "Introduction" here is a technical term for a book which explores some of the basic questions behind the biblical books (such as authorship and sources, manuscript traditions and canonicity) and does so in scholarly detail. These introductory questions need this type of weighty consideration as far as the serious Bible student and scholar are concerned, but are hardly to be recommended to the beginning Bible reader.

Two magazines also recommend themselves to the beginner, while having much to offer the more experienced biblical reader. *The Bible Today* (Liturgical Press, Collegeville, Minnesota) often centres an issue around a particular book, presenting articles which are up-to-date, informative and non-technical. *Scripture in Church* (Dominican Publications, Dublin) is geared more to the liturgical readings and is ideally suited to those who wish to deepen their appreciation of the readings at Mass. It also includes useful articles on biblical topics, often related to the themes of a liturgical season or to biblical books which have a particular prominence in the lectionary during a given time.

Readers who are interested in short essays on biblical topics might turn to *The Bible Now* (Paul Burns and John Cumming, editors, Gill & Macmillan, 1981) to find articles on a variety of subjects such as "The Bible and Liturgy" and "The Ethics of the Old Testament". Patrick Rogers has edited a collection of essays selected from the first few years of the aforementioned *Scripture in Church* entitled *Sowing the Word* (Dominican Publications, 1983); the writings in this later volume tend to be more specific in their subject matter and given in smaller doses than the articles in *The Bible Now*. Either volume would give the reader a good sampling of different approaches and different topics.

All of the above-mentioned books and magazines come from the Catholic tradition of biblical scholarship. There are many good things produced from the Protestant traditions as well, of course. There is, for example, William Neil's *One Volume Bible Commentary* (Hodder and Stoughton, 1962, 1973) which would hardly answer every question a reader would have about every passage, but which offers useful insights into every book in the Bible.

Or one might look at Robert C. Walton's *A Basic Introduction to the Old Testament* and *A Basic Introduction to the New Testament* (SCM, 1980 — a rare example of a biblical introduction really meaning an introduction). These two books are collections of essays on biblical topics, slightly heavier reading than some of the other material recommended in these pages, but full of good things.

Finally, an impassioned plea: never let your reading about the Bible detract from your reading of the Bible itself. The surest way to come to understand and appreciate the message of Scripture is by constant exposure to the biblical text, and the best writings on the Bible are the ones which make us hungry for the Word of God and which lead us to partake of it more deeply. May every reader of this book both know the joy of that hunger and the pleasure of satisfying it at Scripture's rich feast.

Index

(MAJOR REFERENCES ARE GIVEN IN BOLD TYPE)